Now That I'm Out, What Do I Do?

NOW THAT I'M OUT, WHAT DO I DO?

BRIAN McNAUGHT

ST. MARTIN'S PRESS ❧ NEW YORK

Library of Congress Cataloging-in-Publication Data

McNaught, Brian.
Now that I'm out, what do I do? / by Brian McNaught.—1st ed.
p. cm.
Includes bibliographical references.
ISBN 0-312-15616-2
1. Coming out (Sexual orientation)—United States.
2. Gays—United States—Identity.
3. Lesbians—United States—Identity.
4. Gay men—United States—Psychology.
5. Lesbians—United States—Psychology.
I. Title.
HQ76.3.U5M395   1997
305.9'0664—dc21
96-53513
CIP

First Edition: May 1997

1 3 5 7 9 10 8 6 4 2

For my brother, Tommy

CONTENTS

ACKNOWLEDGMENTS

———

A simple though often repeated "thank you" hardly seems adequate to express my enormous gratitude to the loyal family of friends who read, edited, and offered invaluable suggestions for improvements in the manuscript of this book.

The first to see each chapter was, of course, Ray Struble, my life partner, who consistently praised me and encouraged me to believe that every word I wrote was a gem. With such unwavering support, I was prepared for the more critical analysis I wanted and trusted I would receive from my brother and communication specialist, Tommy, and from my dear friend and business partner, Pam Wilson. They had no trouble, I'm grateful to say, in crossing out entire paragraphs and leaving in the margin messages such as "I don't get it."

Wanting the book to be as inclusive as possible, I asked my lesbian soul sister and multitalented friend Bianca Cody Murphy to read with a critical eye for language and examples, as she has two of my prior manuscripts. My good friend and fellow corporate trainer Gary Adkins did the same, as well as challenging me often to dig deeper into my feelings.

I also asked for and received critically important guidance from friends and colleagues Peggy Brick, Amelia Craig, Grant Jahenke, Kevin Jennings, Eric Marcus, Jed Mattes, Paul Shanley, Bill Stayton, David Struble, and Evan Wolfson.

Finally, the manuscript reflects the highly valued input from my editor at St. Martin's Press, Keith Kahla; my copy editor, Janet Fletcher; and my literary agent, John Ware.

Thank you all for your gifts of time, interest, attention, and encouragement. As I trust you each understand, this book is a much clearer, more inclusive, and more thoughtful offering because of you.

INTRODUCTION

As I watched over a hundred thousand people carrying a multi-tude of messages march by during a recent New York City Gay Pride parade, I once again marveled at our community's incredible growth and diversity.

My own "coming out" parade was in Detroit in 1974 for which there were so few people that we had to stay on the sidewalks and wait for the "walk" sign before crossing each street. Back then, some people carried signs designating themselves as *homophiles,* and our chant was "Two, four, six, eight. / Gay is just as good as straight!"

Compare that to the 1993 March on Washington, where there were so many gay, lesbian, bisexual, transgender, and hetero-sexual people assembled that the final contingent of marchers had to stand for hours waiting their turn to join in the parade. When they finally entered the rally site at the end of the day, their hilarious and good-natured chant was "We're tired. We're queer. And we've got attitude!" Snap.

A lot has changed in the gay community in the last twenty years. In fact, for many people it's no longer the *gay* community that gathers for the annual parade, but rather the *gay, lesbian, bisexual,* and *transgender* communities. For some, it's simply the *queer* community. And if *I* think things have changed a lot from when I joined the gay civil rights struggle, pioneers from the 1950s such as Del Martin and Phyllis Lyon, Harry Hay, and Jim Kepner, among others, have stories to tell about conditions surrounding their coming out that really underscore how far we've come.

Most of us would agree that, with the exception of the devastation wrought by AIDS, life today is immensely better for gay people as a result of our hard work, our courage, and our commitment to growth. Society as a whole is more sophisticated about sexual orientation than ever before. There are more protections of our civil rights, fewer legal restrictions on our sexual behaviors, and far more resources available to support us in the development of our identities. Obviously, we have a long, long way to go before the majority of people quit valuing heterosexuality as nature's sole intention and quit narrowly defining "acceptable" gender roles. But we're making progress, one day at a time.

One can only imagine what life will be like for gay people twenty years from now. Perhaps, by then, discrimination based upon sexual orientation will be prohibited at the federal level. Perhaps all state sodomy laws will be rescinded and all public schools will have support systems for gay, lesbian, bisexual, and transgender youth. And perhaps not.

What hasn't changed and probably never will change is our very human desire to feel secure in ourselves and in society. As social creatures, we long for the happiness we associate with belonging in the family, among our friends, at work, and in our worshipping communities.

The letters I get today from gay people are not all that different from the ones I got back in 1974. Nor, I suspect, are they different from the ones that will be written in 2020. Gay people of all ages speak about their hunger for a safe, meaningful place for themselves in the world.

This book is about my personal search for such a place, the remarkable people I've met along the way, and the important lessons I've learned in the process. I feel much different about myself as a gay man and more integrated into the world today than I did twenty years ago, not so much because society has changed, but because I have changed. My observations about that change are offered here in the hope that they might comfort and encourage other hungry travelers.

In my attempt to be as readable and relevant to as broad an

audience as possible, I asked for help from a terrific group of friends with diverse perspectives. I've come to acknowledge that I am but a crude link in the evolutionary chain. I do my best to both accept and go beyond the limitations imposed by the historic, cultural context in which I find myself, but I need all the help I can get to do so.

Yet, even given our combined efforts to be inclusive, I know that some readers may still have trouble relating to some of my words describing this journey. They might wish, for instance, that I had used the word *queer* instead of the cumbersome "gay, lesbian, bisexual, and transgender." Some lesbian women, I suspect, will be disappointed that I use *gay* as a generic term for gay, lesbian, and bisexual. And one friend said that if I wanted to appeal to certain gay men, I should eliminate all references to the Church.

But given all of these possible differences in communication style and perspective, I'm not discouraged, because I know that while all of those issues are important, what's most important to all of us is not so much the words but the music. As one friend reminds me, when we leave a musical or finish listening to a song on the radio, we often can't remember the words we've heard but we certainly remember the music and the powerful feelings it created within us.

The music of this book, I trust, is more timeless than the crude words I employ. It is about finding the truth of our lives from within ourselves and not from outside. Our happiness as human beings is measured by how we feel about ourselves when we walk our journey and not by how many people walk with us, nor by what we call ourselves.

Now That I'm Out, What Do I Do?

ABOUT FITTING INTO THE GAY COMMUNITY

My picture was in the paper when I was twenty-six years old because I was gay[1] and bold, or crazy, enough to say so in 1974. I was a Catholic newspaper reporter and columnist who had just come out to my family and employer.

I didn't know many gay people and had only been to one gay bar, but when the religion editor for *The Detroit News* asked if she could interview me about being gay and Catholic, I said "sure." Only a few months before, I had attempted suicide by drinking a bottle of paint thinner and I was now no longer willing to pretend I was straight.

The day after the interview with me appeared, my newspaper, *The Michigan Catholic*, dropped my column. I was shocked and frightened. The day before the article appeared I was the privileged middle son of a prominent Irish Catholic General Motors family of seven. The next day I was "a homosexual."

CATHOLIC NEWSPAPER DROPS COLUMN BY HOMOSEXUAL proclaimed the eight-column headline in the daily paper. I was no longer Brian, the polite, pleasant, young man who taught religion after work to high school kids; who made people laugh with his good sense of humor; who, at age eighteen, had received the Christian Leadership Award by unanimous vote of his high school faculty. I was "the homosexual," and my name was taken off the award plaque in the high school.

My family members were mostly embarrassed, angry, silent, and hurt. Most of my heterosexual friends were also confounded and upset. At work, all but one of my colleagues signed and publicized a petition decrying my "use of the paper to call attention to" myself.

Then I received an invitation to come to Ann Arbor to speak of my experience to the gay and lesbian student group. I was thrilled but also scared because I didn't know what to expect. Nevertheless, I recall driving excitedly to the University of Michigan campus with the fantasy of being embraced by "my people"—the loving, completely accepting family of my dreams.

"Perhaps I'll finally feel as if I truly *belong*," I thought, reminding myself that in grade school, high school, and college I'd never felt as if I fit in. I had done all the "right" things—played sports, dated, led the pep club, crowned the homecoming queen in my capacity as senior class president, and edited the university yearbook. I was "in" with the in-crowd—but I always felt out of it. Moreover, I generally felt ashamed because of my lack of "normal" erotic feelings for women and terrified that my "dirty little secret" of being attracted to men would be discovered.

But those days were over, I now assured myself. No more hiding my sexual feelings as if they were dirty. No more shame for being different. And the prize for coming out of my closet and announcing to the world that I was gay was that I would finally know the feeling of being welcomed *just as I am.*

Or so I thought.

There was a chill in the student union room on the hot spring day that I came to speak. To my great disappointment, I got the immediate impression that some of the gay students didn't like me.

"You're dressed too nicely," I was told privately. Everyone else was in blue jeans, the uniform of the revolution. I came as the guest speaker, dressed up in shirt, tie, blue blazer, slacks, and loafers.

"Next time I'll wear jeans," I promised myself, feeling very self-conscious about my clothes.

More nervous now, but still very excited, I stood up to cautious applause and began to tell the gathering the story of how and why my award-winning column had been dropped. My stand in battle, I hoped, would earn me a comfortable niche in this important new group.

Just as I began to speak, the door to the room flew open and, amid whistles, cheers, and some rolling of eyes, in marched a bearded man in a wedding dress and veil. He was followed in procession by three men wearing mustaches and pigtails and dressed as bridesmaids. With smiles and waves of "hello" and "sorry, we're late" to me and to the crowd, they took their seats on the floor directly in front of me.

The room was silent again save the whispered observation of one bridesmaid to another about my attire. "Get a load of her," he said.

As I swallowed hard and stumbled into my first few words, I remember thinking to myself, "Oh my God! Now that I'm out, what do I do?" The people assembled in that room were my new family, to be embraced as replacements for my heterosexual family and friends. I was frightened and depressed.

Clearly there were many wonderful people in that room with

whom I might have immediately made good friends. In fact, a colleague and dear friend of mine today assures me with laughter that in 1974 he could have been one of the bridesmaids, or at the very least would have been orchestrating the wedding procession. What I saw through my unsophisticated new gay lenses was a roomful of "them" I mistakenly assumed were all the same, whom I decided I didn't like, and who, I was sure, didn't like me. Once again, I didn't fit in.

I know there are lots of gay men, lesbian women, and bisexual people who can relate to my experience. Though we come from every imaginable background, we share the childhood sense that our sexual and romantic feelings disqualify us from membership in the heterosexual world of our family and friends. When we come out of the closet, most of us lose our status in the straight world. Nevertheless, we believe that once we make contact with the gay, lesbian, and bisexual communities, our isolation and our feelings of second-class status will end.

But for many of us, regrettably, our isolation doesn't end, and for some of us there's a sense of a new second-class status. In my life as an openly gay man, I've received hundreds of letters from strangers and had countless conversations with friends who are frustrated by their feelings of not belonging in the gay community. And many of them are at a loss for what to do.

"I think I'm missing the gay gene," one will say with exasperation. "I don't know why, but I'm just not into . . .," another will admit almost apologetically. "I seem to be too. . . ." "I just can't get comfortable with. . . ."

Some gay people I know even confess to worrying sometimes that other gay people might confront them with the accusation, "You're not *really* gay!" or "You're not *really* a lesbian!"

The truth is, after more than twenty years of being out and very active in gay social, spiritual, and political life, I still feel as if I don't completely fit in. One difference for me today is that I no longer expect to. And it's okay that I don't fit in.

I have been too Catholic for some and too disrespectful of the

Church for others. I'm too butch for some gay people and too femme for others. I'm too radical for some and too conservative for others. I'm too out for some gay people and, believe it or not, too closeted for others. (My parents are rolling in their graves!) After many years of seeking it, I now accept that I will never get the universal "Gay Seal of Approval." Furthermore, I now understand that it doesn't exist.

"But isn't there a test to prove that you're *really* gay?"

No, it's actually a question to determine if you're really *homosexual*. It is: Are you exclusively or predominantly attracted both emotionally and sexually to people of the same gender?

After that, the debate begins. Though no one agrees on how to make further distinctions, some people insist there are a lot more questions still to be answered correctly to prove that one is not just homosexual but truly *gay* or *lesbian.*

"Surely, you have done drag!"

Don't call me Shirley, and no, I have not. What's more, I like opera but I don't *adore* it. When I hear someone mention Special K, I think of a cereal and not a drug. I have no pecs to speak of, and I don't like the pain I experience during, and therefore don't engage in, receptive anal sex.

"Don't go on!"

I must. I have never finished reading *A Boy's Own Story.* S/M scares me, and some drag queens intimidate me. I have no body part that is pierced, I don't do much camp, and I don't think that "bitchy" humor is particularly funny.

"You've gone too far!"

I'm not done. I've only been to the baths once in my life and I walked around for forty-five minutes. I've never fully understood the fascination with Judy Garland (though I love *The Wizard of Oz*)—and—are you ready?—I *hate* the word "queer."

"He's straight!" "He's unliberated!" "He's an assimilationist!"

The truth is I'm still just as "gay" as anyone else. I'm also just as proud of being gay and I'm just as feared and hated as anyone else who is homosexual. But I now feel more comfortable experiencing and expressing being gay *my own way*. I only wish that it hadn't taken me so long and I wish it hadn't caused me so much pain to learn to do so. I also regret and apologize for any pain that I caused others with *my* expectations of *them* as gay people.

During gay and lesbian pride marches, we often point our fingers at people holding anti-gay signs, or at church or government buildings, and yell in unison, "Shame, shame, shame." It feels good to make such loud public pronouncements about other people's inappropriate behavior. But it doesn't feel so good when it's done to you. Regrettably, some of us also angrily point at each other with the intention of creating shame and forcing compliance with preconceived notions of what it means to be gay.

For many years, I did feel some shame because I believed that I wasn't gay enough. I feared I might be discovered as an impostor, kicked out of the group, and left with no community to which I could turn.

Now, I feel more relaxed about my style of being gay and I've found my niche in the world. What I've finally learned is that the key to my happiness is in knowing, loving, and being myself—not in knowing, loving, and being what others expect of me.

For instance, I'm fascinated by and generally enjoy seeing gay men in drag, and at the same time I know it's not for me, at least not today. I love good gay camp humor, but I'm lousy at it. I affirm the rights of others to enjoy all forms of consensual sexual pleasuring, but I know that some behaviors aren't right for me now and perhaps never will be.

I think some men look great with an earring, and a ring through the nipple on a well-developed chest can be a real turn-on for me, but I'm not ready to pierce anything. I listen in awe as cofounders Tom Reilly and Karen Wickre describe the critically important computer networking efforts of Digital Queers. On them, "queer" works. On me, it doesn't, for now.

My happiness results when I find out and live what works for me today. I'm also happiest when I accept that what works for me will not necessarily work for everyone who is gay, lesbian or bisexual. Not knowing this truth, when I entered my new life as an openly gay person, caused me many years of heartache.

At the end of the tumultuous day during which the people of Michigan read and heard that I was gay, a closeted homosexual I knew sat in his car across the street and repeatedly screamed "faggot" at me as I headed into the office parking lot. It scared and hurt me. It also angered me.

At the time I didn't understand why he did it. Today I feel he screamed at me because he was frightened and angry, and perhaps ashamed. I think he saw my coming out as a statement about his being closeted. ("Outing" is the same phenomenon but from the other side of the closet door.) Some people get angry when others make choices that are different from their own. He and I both did.

During my subsequent hunger strike, when I was sustained by only water in an attempt to get the Catholic Church to educate the clergy about homosexuality, I was crushed to learn that some gay Catholics were very angry at me for confronting the bishops. They wrote or called to insist that I stop embarrassing them. At the time, I was deeply hurt, disappointed, and angry that their fear of the bishops and their desire to be left alone were such high priorities for them. If anyone was going to be my ally, I thought, gay Catholics should be!

The truth is, many gay Catholics *were* my allies. The national office of Dignity, the organization for gay Catholics, for instance, was very supportive of my efforts. Those members who opposed me felt there should be only one gay Catholic position. I did too. I made the mistake of expecting everyone to believe and behave as I did. I wanted them to feel shame for what I perceived to be their cowardice.

Shortly thereafter, when I was Dignity's national director of social action, I was invited to give a presentation at a regional gay leadership conference in Philadelphia. My workshop focused on effective ways to educate religious institutions about gay issues.

Among the members of the audience was a local group of "radical queens" whose reported purpose was to "trash" my talk. Because I was Catholic, they assumed I would defend the writings of Saint Paul. They wanted to shame me.

"What do you have to say about Saint Paul?" yelled out one of the members of the group as I began to speak.

"He wasn't writing about homosexuality as we understand it," I answered. "He was condemning behaviors associated with temple prostitution. But even if he was condemning same-sex behavior, Saint Paul wrote many things that Catholics in good conscience ignore."

I passed their test. They got up and walked out, but I was hurt and enraged. How dare they! I ate, drank, and slept gay civil rights. I had lost my job for being gay. I lived on occasional contributions and on the pittance I made from my column in the gay press and from speaking engagements. "What do you have to do to belong to this club?" I fumed.

My mistake was in wanting to be accepted by *everyone* who was gay and assuming that if I paid my dues, everyone would embrace me. I hungered for approval. I craved a sense of security that I truly belonged.

So too, I suspect, did the gay men who called themselves radical queens and who came to trash my workshop. They too had undoubtedly felt terribly isolated as children. They longed for a cultural revolution that would destroy everything in society that shamed and marginalized them. They saw me as a defender of the Judeo-Christian ethic and, as such, someone in the way of their revolution.

Generally, when we gay people come out of the closet, we seek a world in which we will never feel shame again. We identify this world as "the gay community." But in the process of building this idealized, substitute family, we often confuse *security* with *conformity.* When other gay people are not being gay in a way that makes us comfortable, out of our insecurity, we sometimes attempt to shame them into our image and likeness, just as some heterosexual bullies did to us.

We may bully other gay, lesbian, or bisexual people or be bullied ourselves over politics, faith, family, relationships, appearance, and even health status.

Lesbian and gay activist authors Urvashi Vaid,[2] Andrew Sullivan,[3] Bruce Bawer,[4] and Michelangelo Signorile,[5] among others, have each published different and sometimes contrary views on who gay people are, where we're going, and how we ought to get there. There is today and seemingly always has been an unsettling tension in the gay political movement. It often feels as if you must march to the beat of one particular drummer or your commitment to gay liberation will be questioned.

Lesbian pioneers Barbara Gittings and Kay Tobin Lahusen, for instance, told me that when a handful of brave gay souls marched in front of the White House during the McCarthy era, they were criticized by other activists for their attire. The women wore dresses and heels and the men wore suits and ties in their efforts to put an everyday face on homosexuals. They were accused by some of pandering to heterosexual fears.

Lobbyist and Human Rights Campaign founder Steve Endean confided before his death that his most painful memory of community work was being called an Uncle Tom by some people for working within the system on a gay rights bill in Minnesota. Steve's entire adult life was committed to creating a safer world for lesbian women and gay men. Some gay people objected to his working behind the scenes with straight politicians to do so.

The day after it was announced in 1982 that I had been chosen by the mayor of Boston to be his ombudsperson, a small group of disgruntled gay men plastered the city with posters proclaiming: BRIAN MCNAUGHT, THE MAYOR'S LIAISON TO THE GAY COMMUNITY, INVITES YOU TO A PUBLIC ORGY IN THE BOSTON COMMON . . .

BRING TOYS AND BOYS, SLINGS AND THINGS. COSPONSORED BY DIGNITY AND INTEGRITY. They thought the mayor shouldn't have picked someone associated in any way with the Church.

Many gay and lesbian people I know who have made significant contributions to our movement have been hurt by equally disturbing behavior from other gay people who felt angry and threatened by differences. While those differences often center around politics, they can also be more personal.

Some "lipstick lesbians," for instance, feel as if they are not trusted because they like to wear makeup and dress femme. Some lesbians sense they are not completely welcome in the women's community because they have too many close gay male friends or are active in a gay religious group. Some gay women feel ostracized because they don't identify with the labels "lesbian," "dyke," or "queer."

A slightly different set of issues causes the same feelings for gay men. Some feel inadequate because they don't have well-developed chests and washboard stomachs. Others feel they face rejection because they aren't into leather or because they won't do drag. Still others sense disapproval because they're interested in professional sports, can't coordinate colors, or don't embrace the label "faggot."

On one of my early trips to a gay bar, I came directly from work in a coat and tie.

"Check out the tie," insisted one patron to another in an exaggerated tone of disapproval as I entered the bar.

Seeking the acceptance of these seemingly far wiser gay men, I took the tie off. They bullied. I felt shame. I wanted to belong to "the gay family," so I changed. Sometimes, though, you can't change so quickly and easily.

On my first and only trip to a gay bathhouse, I was a nervous wreck because I so wanted to be accepted—no, *embraced*—into what I identified as the gay male erotic brotherhood. My mind was filled with exciting sexual fantasies as I approached the main desk. "Will I meet their standards?" I worried as I entered the locker room.

Two gay men sat on benches reading the local gay newspaper in which my syndicated column appeared. One recognized me from the picture that accompanied the column. "Hey, it's him!" I heard him whisper to his friend. I was exhilarated. Feeling terribly shy, I hoped they might start a conversation with me.

"He has no body," his friend replied as I finished undressing.

I had been judged inadequate. I felt ashamed of my body and was certain that I didn't belong in the bathhouse. I didn't fit in.

For years to come, I would look at myself in the mirror and hear the words "He has no body."

"They're right," I would observe. "Look at those arms. Look at that chest. No muscles. No body."

Some bisexual women call themselves lesbians for fear of being rejected as "Lesbian Lite." Some gay men uneasily call each other "queen," "Mary," and "Miss Thing" because they think that is what is expected of them. I started going to the gym in the hope of building an acceptable body.

"But I love your body just the way it is," my life partner, Ray, would protest.

"That's not enough. *They* have to like it," I would say to myself with hungry thoughts of universal gay male approval.

Ray and I are both HIV-negative and are very grateful for our health. Yet, we know of some gay men who feel guilty and almost embarrassed because they are negative. For them, being HIV positive is the litmus test of gay male identity.

All of this makes me very sad. Gay, lesbian, and bisexual people should not continue to feel inadequate after they leave the closet. It's not healthy for the individual, nor for our civil rights movement.

One of the early symbols of gay liberation was the butterfly. Once out of the closet, we argued, we should be able to spread our beautiful wings and fly unencumbered. To do so, though, requires that we let go of the attitudes and the behaviors that keep us from feeling free.

In order to fly, I'm learning to stop letting in the bullying voices of disapproval. I'm learning to let go of my romantic fantasy of, and need for, universal gay acceptance. And I'm learning to identify and accept what makes *me* happy so that I can truly enjoy my life as a gay man.

A few years ago, I recognized that I have a "dis-ease" with myself and with the world that is often called "codependency." That means, among other things, that I'm prone to value other people's feelings, perceptions, wants, and needs more than my own. I grew up not trusting that I was truly loved. As a result, I've often tried to control people's responses to me by second-guessing what they wanted. I believed that I could manipulate my world to ensure that I was safe, if not loved and respected.

Such controlling, manipulative efforts make honest relationships impossible. They also create resentments, because people who try to please rarely know when to stop. We don't know boundaries, either ours or others'. I suspect that quite a few gay people can identify with these feelings.

As a child, I knew intellectually that my parents loved me, but I didn't trust in my heart that they would *really* love me if they knew I was gay. So I began to second-guess what they wanted from me. I did the same with my teachers, my classmates, and my friends. This dependence on the impossible approval of others eventually led to my suicide attempt. I drank paint thinner and swallowed pills because I was losing control of my life and I wanted to get out before everything fell apart. My secret attraction to men was demanding to be expressed, but I believed the truth about me, if known, would make me unlovable—that I would lose approval. I didn't know how to both be myself and please other people.

I hit bottom when I had my stomach pumped. Though I didn't know about codependency and twelve-step programs of recovery, I knew that I had to make changes in my life. I promised myself as I sat crying on the emergency room table with a tube down my nose and throat that I would never again live my life based upon people's expectations of me.

I meant my promise but I didn't keep it. Low self-esteem is a patient, persistent traveling companion, and it waited for me to let my guard down. That didn't take long.

After I came out, I started doing the same second-guessing with the gay community as I had done with the straight community. I wanted approval and I unconsciously attempted to control gay people's responses to me. "If I do this, will you love me? What about that? Now do I pass the test?"

I tried and tried but, again, it didn't work. It seemed that no matter what I accomplished, I didn't feel secure in gay people's acceptance of me. Once more, I didn't know how to both please other people and be myself.

I hit bottom again a couple of years ago. I remember lying in bed frustrated, angry, and emotionally exhausted as I cried quietly, feeling very alone.

"Does *anybody* really know who I am?" I asked as I reflected on my relationships with my family and friends, on people who had heard me speak or who had read what I had written. "Does even Ray really know me?"

"How could they?" I concluded. *"You* don't even know you. What do *you* want? What do *you* feel?"

I realized that I was very unhappy and I decided that I didn't want to live that way any longer. My first step toward changing my life was acknowledging that I had a dysfunctional way of experiencing myself and the world. Doing so lifted an enormous burden from my heart.

Through therapy, prayer, and hard work I've succeeded in making significant changes in the way I think, feel, and behave as a gay man. As a result, I'm happier today than I have ever been. I'm also more at peace with other gay people.

Reading books such as Melody Beattie's classic *Codependent No More!*[6] was a great help in understanding my issues. Involving myself in a twelve-step recovery program provided me with a source of continual encouragement. I've also benefitted greatly from Ray's support and role-modeling, and that of family members and friends.

Lots of gay, lesbian, and bisexual people today are privately exploring whether they're happy in the way they relate to themselves, to other gay people, and to the rest of the world. Many of them are benefiting from examining in more detail the impact of their formative years on their current attitudes and behaviors.

I've met only a few gay men and lesbians who say they never doubted the love of their parents. Most gay people I know say they feared the love was conditional on their being heterosexual. Such feelings undermine children's ability to trust they are lovable, particularly when they grow up in a world in which their sexual feelings are described as "sick," "sinful," and "unnatural."

It would be wonderful if, when we entered into the gay community, we automatically shed those feelings of inadequacy and trusted that we were good just the way we were, but often we don't. Old ways of seeing the world die hard, particularly when reinforced by other walking-wounded people.

For lots of gay people, this dis-ease with themselves and the world means feeling anxious, self-conscious, defensive, inadequate, angry, ashamed, and resentful. These feelings can lead to a variety of unhealthy and inappropriate behaviors, such as excessive drinking and drugging, compulsive sexual activity, risky sexual conduct, the hostile outing of others, biting sarcasm, and unrealistic expectations of ourselves and others about what it means to be *truly* gay.

When people begin "recovery" from old ways of thinking, they question the healthiness and usefulness of their attitudes and behaviors. They ask themselves questions such as "How do *I* feel?" "What do *I* want?" "What does it mean to *me* to be gay?" "What does it mean to me to be male/female?" and "How do I want to spend the rest of my life?"

14

For most gay people, such questioning will result in coming out to their families so that they can start building honest relationships. It may also mean coming out to their bosses or changing jobs so that they can be themselves at work. Gay people who grow in self-esteem generally leave unhappy heterosexual marriages or unhappy, unhealthy homosexual relationships. Some people will quit drinking and others will swear off drugs. Some gay people will make changes in their sexual behavior. Once in this process, gay people begin striving to be true to themselves regardless of what others think.

If, for instance, today I hear "Check out the tie," I don't immediately assume that the person is talking about *my* tie, that it is a criticism, or that, if it is a criticism, it has any particular merit.

When I look in the mirror at my body today, I'm often able to think, "You have a *nice* body. It works very well for you. It doesn't look like the bodies in the ads for gay male vacation cruises, but most of the men on those cruises don't look like the ads either. It's a fit and healthy body for a middle-aged man. You should feel proud."

As part of my new way of thinking and being, I now try to avoid people, books, films, magazines, columns, comedy acts, and conferences that are negative or harshly judgmental or that I fear will activate the insecurities of my past. Conversely, I seek out people, places, and things that help me feel good about who I am as a gay person and what I am becoming.

When I start to feel anxious with or resentful of other gay people, I try to remind myself that I can't control the behavior of other people, only my expectations of them. I ask myself, "Am I doing what I'm doing because I *want* to or because I feel I *have* to in order to get approval?" I work to accept that when people criticize, they are judging my *behavior* and not *me*.

I sure wish I had felt like this when I was invited to speak to the University of Michigan gay student group in 1974. If so, I would have first decided if I thought it would be a positive experience for me and a good use of my time. Knowing today how much fun it is to speak with gay and lesbian college students, I'm sure I would have said "yes."

I probably would have worn more casual clothes, though not jeans. When invited to speak, I still like to dress up a little.

The crowd of strangers wouldn't scare me so much this time because I would feel secure in my own experience of being gay. I would talk to as many people as I could, realizing they were not all the same. I now know that I would really like some of the gay people and not be as drawn to others. Some of the people would really like me too. Others wouldn't.

When I started speaking to the group, I would still feel a little nervous and I have accepted performance anxiety as an important ingredient to my success, but I would trust today that what I had to say would be of interest to them.

When the bearded bride and the mustached and pigtailed bridesmaids walked in, I wouldn't look as startled as I did in 1974, and I expect that I would roll my eyes and laugh along with them. Today, I have more affection for the members of my community who have different styles of being gay than me.

In answer to my question, "Now that I'm out, what do I do?" I now say, "Relax. Be yourself. Have some fun, and spread your wings and fly."

2

ABOUT
THE MAN ON THE PLANE

The businessman sitting next to me on the flight home was about my age, but it immediately became clear we had little else in common.

"Heading home?" he asked with a smile as I settled into my place by the window. As sometimes happens on airplanes, we were both open to having a conversation with a stranger.

I soon learned that he lived in Cobb County, Georgia. I felt immediate discomfort and defiance. Cobb County's commissioners had passed a resolution proclaiming that homosexuality was incompatible with their community values.

I also quickly discovered that my companion was a Born Again Christian whose wife was active in the ultraconservative organization Concerned Women for America. He told me that he was a decorated Navy pilot during the Vietnam War. He had been featured in *Life* magazine among other war veterans and had received one of President George Bush's "Thousand Points of Light" awards for his work as an advocate for veterans.

This exceedingly gracious man was also the subject of profiles in *Fortune* and *Inc.* magazines for his entrepreneurial success and was scheduled to share his insights in the next week with twenty-five hundred Born Again businesspeople.

The more questions I asked him, the more personally threatening information I learned. "I can't *believe* this!" I thought. "He's Born Again, he is probably Republican, and he lives in Cobb County. He and his wife are undoubtedly Bible-quoting, private country club homophobes. But he's so *nice!*"

"So, tell me about you," he said. "Are you married? What do you do for work?"

"I help corporations address homophobia in the workplace," I said as matter-of-factly as I could. "My partner, Ray, and I have been together for almost twenty years."

We smiled nervously at each other for a quiet second. I can imagine the images that flashed through his mind as I told him that I was gay. I can also imagine that he thought to himself, "But he's so *nice!*"

"So, what exactly do you do in these corporations?" he asked.

"I help the heterosexual employees understand the impact on productivity of anti-gay behavior. I begin by restating the company's policy that all employees will be evaluated on their skills and performance, not on their sexual orientation, or their race, religion, age, or gender," I explained. "Then I describe inappropriate behaviors, such as telling 'fag' jokes or posting judgmental biblical quotes on bulletin boards."

He smiled in recognition that such things could happen.

"I then remind the employees that they are entitled to their personal values and that the company insists only that they be mutually respectful," I said.

He nodded in agreement. "I'm amazed that corporations care enough about it to bring someone like you in. Does it help?" he asked.

Sensing his genuine interest, I told him stories of dramatic changes in the behavior and attitudes of some employees. "Most people who tell jokes and use offensive language generally have no idea of the impact of their behavior," I said. "I help them understand by explaining what it means to be gay. When they understand who they're hurting, they're less inclined to behave in hostile ways."

"How do you help them know what it means to be gay?" he asked after some silence.

"I explain what we know about the causes of sexual orientation, that it's not a *choice,*" I said with emphasis. "I take them through a powerful role-reversal guided imagery during which they imagine growing up with a secret they're afraid to share with anyone for fear of losing love and respect. Probably, though, the most powerful thing I do is tell them my story. I tell them about what my life was like as the middle child in a family of seven Irish Catholics, a child who grew up wanting to be a saint but who also was aware that he was 'different.' "

He seemed intrigued. "What *was* it like?" he asked.

There was a time in my life I would have been too afraid of or too angry at the man sitting next to me to tell him about my life. I would have feared his rejection or been angry at him for his heterosexual privilege and for all of the horrible things that have been done throughout history by straight men to gay men and women.

Though I could still feel fear and anger, I also felt confidence in my ability to survive a hostile response, and hopeful about my fellow passenger's ability to become an ally. And so, I told him my story. As I spoke, he occasionally smiled with recognition. He also furrowed his brow with intense interest. Sometimes he seemed to withdraw with apprehension, but then he would reengage with clarifying questions and encourage me on.

"The horror of growing up gay," I explained, "is having a secret you don't understand and are afraid to share with your family and friends for fear of losing their love and respect."

He offered that he had children and had always assumed they were heterosexual. I told him that while it was probable that they were, it couldn't be guaranteed. "One way or the other, you don't influence their orientation. You only influence whether or not they'll tell you they're gay."

I told him about the alarming numbers of gay teenagers who kill themselves or run away because of their secret. I explained how growing up gay was different from growing up black or Latino, in that gay kids have straight parents who assume their children are straight and treat them accordingly.

"A black child can tell his parents that he's been beaten up for being black. A gay kid won't report the fight," I said. Then I gave him examples of how a father can emotionally abuse his gay son without knowing it.

"Imagine being a thirteen-year-old gay youth, riding with your dad in the car on the way to a ball game. The disc jockey on the radio tells a 'fag' joke. You look over at Dad and see that he's laughing. You say to yourself, 'I'll never tell him my secret.' "

The pained look on his face told me that he understood.

He and I were the same age. That made it easier for him to put himself in my shoes as I described joining the Scouts, dating, playing ball, getting elected class president, editing the yearbook, and landing my first job. He remembered the events but admitted that he didn't know the feelings of isolation, alienation, fear, shame, and confusion I described as part of growing up with a secret I couldn't share with my father or mother.

We laughed together at our funny reflections of being teenagers. He too recalled the special allure that mouseketeer Annette Funicello had for most boys. He grimaced when he heard that my high school guidance counselor told our class, "If you boys tell me that you've screwed a chick, I'll talk to you. Tell me you're queer and I'll kick you out of my office."

"Did you like girls?" he asked.

"Sure. I had girl friends from first grade on. I loved them," I explained, "but I didn't feel anything sexual for them. I tried. In college I bought a six-pack of beer and a massage book, and I had my first heterosexual experience with the woman in the apartment next door. Nothing."

He laughed and then asked, "Did you try again or did you never have the urge?"

My smile answered his question.

He marveled at my success as a Catholic reporter, columnist, and occasional talk show host. "Your folks must have been proud."

He looked away as I related my attempt at suicide with turpentine and pills. "I was so tired of the isolation, the fear, the guilt and shame that came from living a lie," I explained.

My companion asked me about how my family reacted to my being gay and he asked about my relationship with God.

I told him my family initially had a hard time but were now very supportive. I described how my 101-year-old grandmother once retired to her bedroom where she listened with interest, and some pride, to me being interviewed on her favorite radio program. I told him about my mom weeping when I came out because she feared the world would treat me poorly, and about how Dad thought I had a hormone imbalance that I'd outgrow.

I told him that my very important relationship with God was healthy and happy, though I no longer belonged to an organized church. I also described in more detail my loving relationship with Ray.

When I finished, we sat in silence. Then, as we approached Atlanta, the man sitting next to me said with a gentle smile, "Brian, as sure as I'm sitting here, I believe that God had you sit next to me.

"My wife and I write lots of checks to groups that oppose civil rights for homosexuals," he explained, "but the truth is we don't know any homosexuals. You've put a face on this issue, and I won't ever forget that. I can't tell you how this is going to impact what I say to those twenty-five hundred businessmen I'm addressing next week, but I know it will. I also know this is going to be harder for my wife. She wasn't here with us, but I'll surely tell her about it."

With that, the Born Again Christian, middle-aged veteran, Republican businessman from Cobb County, Georgia, reached into his briefcase and pulled out a dog-eared copy of the *Life* magazine in which he was featured, and he gave it to me. "I want you to have this," he said.

"You shouldn't give me that," I protested.

"I want to," he said. "It's important."

"Will you then take a copy of my book?" I asked as I reached for a copy of *On Being Gay.*

"If you'll inscribe it," he replied.

We have not talked since, though I did write him a letter in which I said how grateful I was that we had met and had both dared to stretch beyond our levels of comfort. I suggested that we had entered the sacred ground of mutual respect and acceptance. I don't know if our encounter had a long-term effect on him. It did on me.

Though I continue to fume at the anti-gay rhetoric of the religious right's leadership and resent the fear I have living in such an atmosphere of intolerance, I don't believe, as I once did, that all religious conservatives are alike. I have a face, now one of a growing few, of a Born Again Christian who was decent, loving, open, and honest. I suspect I had the same effect upon him.

If so, if I shook up his preconceived ideas about gay, lesbian, and bisexual people, it happened because I did more than tell him that I was gay. I helped him understand what it *means* to be gay by telling him my story.

Simply coming out is not enough. We have to go beyond it.

By "coming out" I mean telling someone that we are gay. Fortunately, lots of gay people have come out, alerting many heterosexuals to the fact that there are homosexuals in their circle of family, friends, and work associates. Unfortunately, the heterosexuals we tell generally don't know what we're talking about. They often don't know what it means to be gay, lesbian, or bisexual because we gay people usually don't elaborate.

We just say "I'm gay!" We then assume that straight people have the ability to figure out for themselves the meaning and significance of our disclosure. We hope they'll immediately understand, but they don't. We hope they'll instantly love and respect us just the same as they did before we told them, but generally they won't.

Without the benefit of explanation, what heterosexuals often think we've just told them is, "We have sex differently than you do." Beyond the very unpleasant and unsettling "pornographic" images that frequently result, the straight person often then leaps to a variety of assumptions based upon the unflattering images of homosexuals he or she has stored since childhood. These provocative stereotypes have been reinforced by carefully selected pictures of Gay Pride marchers, broadcast on their televisions and printed in their newspapers.

"Gay" to many, if not most, uninformed heterosexuals typically means unnatural, immoral sex by sissy boys who want to be women and mannish women who hate men. "Gay" can mean to them "outrageous" public behavior, sin, strangers who stalk children, and painful, early, shameful death.

The heterosexuals who think this way are most often not mean-spirited people who want to believe the worst about someone who is gay. They are, for the most part, terribly misinformed and therefore frightened. At least, that is my experience.

To help heterosexuals get in touch with their stereotypes and with their fear of gay people, I have members of my corporate audience imagine other people thinking of them as gay.

"You're all getting a copy of my book *(Gay Issues in the Workplace)* as part of this workshop," I will say. "Imagine yourself on an airplane. Please pull the book out and put it on your lap. Leave it there, cover side up, for a moment."

Nervous laughter.

"The person sitting next to you is looking over to see what you're reading. What does he or she assume about you."

"That I'm gay," several people will say.

"That's right. How do you feel about that?"

Silence.

"You just sneezed," I say to a man in the second row. "What's the person sitting next to you thinking now?"

"AIDS," answers the man. "I have AIDS and now they're going to get it."

"That's right," I say. "How do you like having people be afraid of you because they assume you have AIDS and are going to infect them?"

Silence.

"There's no leg room on these planes, is there?" I say to a man sitting in the third row. "You change your sitting position and accidently bump the knee of the guy sitting next to you. What's he thinking?"

"That I'm coming on to him," replies the man.

"Right," I say. "They think you're gay, and they assume you are automatically interested in them. What else does the person sitting next to you think about you?"

"That I have no religion," calls out one woman.

"That I molest children," adds another.

"Pretty scary stuff," I say. "Do you think he or she imagines that you are in a loving, committed relationship? That you would be a good neighbor? That perhaps you served in the Armed Forces?"

Silence.

"How do you feel having people think you're gay?"

Silence.

"It's all the stereotypes they have of you that make you so uncomfortable, isn't it?" I ask. "You don't like them assuming horrible things about you. I know. Neither do I. That's why it's always so hard for me to tell people that I'm gay. I don't like the horrible things that some folks assume about me."

People in the workshop nod in recognition, with a new awareness.

Seeing people's attitudes change is very exciting. But it should frighten every gay, lesbian, and bisexual person that the majority of heterosexual people are so terribly misinformed about homosexuality. I used to think that if heterosexuals merely learned that famous people they respected were gay or lesbian, they would abandon their negative stereotypes about all other homosexuals. But I discovered that while they may be shocked to learn that Tchaikovsky was homosexual, uninformed heterosexuals often decide one of two things. Either the composer was an exception or he too was a horrible person and is no longer worthy of respect.

"Horrible person? What about me?" gay people often then ask painfully. "How can my family and friends maintain all of those frightening thoughts about homosexuals knowing me as they do?" Yet, upon hearing that a loved one is gay, some family members and friends will also respond, "You're not like those other homosexuals" or "I'm not sure I *do* know you."

Regrettably, outing famous people who are gay will not change our everyday world into the safe, loving, respectful, gay-positive environment we seek. Neither will it be much affected by our simply coming out, even if everyone who is gay turned lavender overnight. Heterosexual family members, friends, and coworkers still wouldn't understand, any more than they can understand, without the benefit of education, what it means to be a member of a racial minority in this culture.

More than announce that we are gay—more than proclaim *what* we are—gay, lesbian, and bisexual people need to come forth with explanations of *who* we are.

I explain that being gay, for me, means being physically and emotionally attracted exclusively or predominantly to members of my own gender. It means experiencing enormous physical, psychological, and spiritual pleasure when I relate sexually to a man with whom I share affection and attraction. Being gay means acknowledging and embracing my feelings and behavior and integrating them into the rest of my life.

But such integration is easier said than done. Heterosexuals need to know that because of the culture in which we live, being gay means growing up with unexplained feelings of arousal in a world that finds such feelings disgusting, abnormal, and sinful. For me that meant growing up feeling isolated, lonely, fearful, guilty, ashamed, and confused. Heterosexuals need to know that because I grew up with a socially determined "terrible" secret, my interactions with family, friends, teachers, and colleagues were dramatically affected. I felt that no one understood me. I felt like a phony who one day would be discovered. I didn't trust that anyone did or could truly love me as I was.

To any casual observer, even to a hostile one, it should be very clear that understanding my sexual orientation requires much more than knowing what I do in bed. Being gay has impacted every moment of my life since I first became aware of my feelings, and perhaps even before. It has affected my spirituality, my relationships, and my work.

When heterosexuals are educated by gay people who tell their stories, they begin to understand that their frightening stereotypes and impressions are not factual. I don't know how long the insights last. Repeated positive contact with an emotionally healthy, happy gay man or lesbian woman and with accurate information is essential to unraveling years of negative impressions and fears. That's why we have to keep telling our stories to anyone who will listen.

Most gay people understand the powerful impact that coming out has on one's life. They know that coming out is essential for one's mental and physical health. The closet guarantees emotional death. I know of no gay man or lesbian woman who regrets coming out, only the years it took to do so.

Beyond the powerful personal rewards, we know there are also undeniable political benefits. Every study underscores how heterosexual people who know gay people are far more likely to support efforts, such as legislation, that value and protect gay people. The truth of this is beautifully summed up in a sign Ray and I photographed as we exited the nature conservatory in Barbados.

Quoting African conservationist Baba Dioum, the sign read: IN THE END WE WILL CONSERVE ONLY WHAT WE LOVE AND RESPECT. WE WILL LOVE ONLY WHAT WE UNDERSTAND. WE WILL UNDERSTAND ONLY WHAT WE ARE TAUGHT OR ALLOWED TO EXPERIENCE.

"I didn't understand before today what it's like being gay," person after person will say following a presentation on gay issues. "I have a brother who's gay but he's never told me what it was like," one says. "I have a daughter who's a lesbian but she's never shared with me what it was like growing up gay," offers another.

If we are to be loved and respected by others, we have to enable them to understand who we are by telling them what it's like.

With so much to gain then, both personally and politically, what stops gay, lesbian, and bisexual people from coming out and telling our stories to anyone who will listen? Why do even those of us who consider ourselves out of the closet often duck personal questions when we know that truthful responses will both liberate us and change the attitudes and behavior of others? Why do we continue to hide who we are from cab drivers, classmates, electricians, door-to-door salespeople, secretaries, great-uncles, and fellow passengers on airplanes?

There are three basic reasons for our behavior: our heterosexism, our homophobia, and our heterophobia.

HETEROSEXISM

Most gay, lesbian, and bisexual people grow up assuming that all other people are straight and believing that it's better to be straight than gay. With the help of the culture, we believe there *is* something queer about being gay and we think that every straight person will hate us.

Tragically, many of us continue to think this way. We thus find it very difficult to feel safe, loved, and respected as a homosexual and therefore choose not to come out.

Heterosexism is not just the assumption that everyone is heterosexual unless they say or prove otherwise. It's a value system that honors heterosexuality as God's intention for humans and degrades homosexuality as a poor substitute. Not unlike racism, sexism, and the other isms that judge one gender, race, religion, age, physical characteristic, etc., to be superior to others, heterosexism makes gay people second-class for life.

Many gay, lesbian, and bisexual people make everyday decisions about their lives based upon a heterosexist value system. For example, we refrain from engaging in even appropriate signs of public affection, such as holding the hand of or kissing the lips of our partner in life, because it might offend heterosexual people. Heterosexism prompts gay people both to assume that the hotel housekeeper is straight and that she or he would be offended by the sight of a gay book or periodical left in the room. We often therefore "straighten up" the room before we depart for the day. We also straighten up our conduct in all public places.

Our internalized heterosexism has us assuming that everyone attending our class reunion is heterosexual and believing that if we're going to go to the reunion, or to the wedding or the office party, we ought to have the common decency not to impose our depraved, understandably upsetting behavior on the good, decent, moral heterosexuals who are going to be there, especially if they are young or elderly. In other words, come alone, keep quiet, and don't ask anyone of the same sex to dance.

HOMOPHOBIA

Add to this sad attitude our homophobia and we have even more of a reason to keep our secret to ourselves. Homophobia is a mind set in which lesbian or gay sex is seen as dirty, selfish, disgusting, compulsive, and immoral. Gay people are seen as all of the above as well as immature, confused, unreliable, and outrageous.

Many gay people internalize this social construct. Some, therefore, have little sympathy for people who die of AIDS because of "promiscuous" sex, yet speak of others as "innocent" victims; shed few tears for those gay people who are beaten up because they undoubtedly "flaunted" their homosexuality and had it coming; and fail to come to the defense of colleagues who are fired for being gay because they were probably "in everybody's face."

Internalized homophobia, which embraces the negative stereotypes of homosexuals as accurate, also prompts some gay people to consistently undercut the achievements of other gay people, to constantly criticize the efforts of the movement's "so-called" leaders, and to harshly challenge the scholarship of gay academics. The unarticulated attitude is, "Who in the hell do they think they are? They're no better than the rest of us. They're just faggots and dykes. Look at 'em pretend they're not queer."

Contrast this to the attitude expressed about a heterosexual actor, writer, parent, politician, or clergyperson who speaks out in behalf of gay people. Such people are often canonized: "Aren't they wonderful!" for not hating us.

If you think your secret is dirty, you're not inclined to tell it.

HETEROPHOBIA

Further, if you angrily decide that your listener is not only heterosexual but also a hostile, Bible-quoting bigot, you're likely to see any effort at human dialogue as a waste of time.

Often in the development of a positive homosexual identity,

gay people go through a hostile, resentful stage during which everyone who is gay is good and everyone who is straight is evil. Vivienne Cass, the Australian psychotherapist who devised a model for "homosexual identity formation,"[1] refers to that stage as "Identity Pride."

Heterophobia, the fear and hatred of heterosexuals, is an unfortunate but predictable component of some people's identity pride. For many of us, at least initially, our pride is more reactive than proactive, and we angrily denounce as an enemy anyone who is straight.

Gay is good because straight is bad. Straight is bad because gay is good. In that mind frame, even if we have mostly overcome our internalized heterosexism and homophobia, talking with heterosexuals about who we are is considered stupid because they all are narrow-minded, judgmental, unliberated oppressors, and "who cares what they think, anyway!" This attitude has led to strong, vocal condemnation by some gay and lesbian people of the efforts by other gay and lesbian people to work with or to educate heterosexuals.

Cass observes that this us-versus-them mentality works only until the gay person encounters a heterosexual who challenges his or her negative stereotypes.

I was in this stage of development when I sat next to a nun on an airplane. In my briefcase was a gay book I had brought along to read. As usual, I was confronted with a dozen conflicted feelings about reading a gay book in public. My heterosexism, homophobia, and heterophobia did battle with my gay pride call to arms. This time, my frustration with and anger at the Catholic Church also came into play.

"I'm going to read this book and if she sees it and doesn't like it, that's *her* problem," I defiantly decided.

Out came my book, which I held on my lap for a prolonged

period of time as I continuously reread the title and processed the conflicted feelings that arose.

"OK, open it up. What's she thinking? I don't care what she's thinking. Where was I? What page? What paragraph? That looks familiar. No, I think I just read that. I can't believe how the Church let me down. I wonder if any of the nuns who taught me in school have followed my career. I wonder what they'd say. I don't care what they'd say. Where was I?"

By the end of the flight I had not read and comprehended much more than I had at the beginning. Yet, I had made my point, hadn't I? I would not be bullied by a representative of the Church! As I was defiantly pulling my things together, the nun handed me a note. It read, "I support what you are doing. Bless you."

I felt sad, confused, happy, and ashamed. "I made her my enemy because of her clothing," I thought. "Was she a lesbian? Why would she need to be a lesbian in order to be supportive? I wish I had talked with her."

Similar encounters continued to create similarly conflicted feelings in me for many years.

A few years ago I was on my way to a speaking engagement in Vermont. The car sent by the school to transport me from the airport broke down in a snowstorm. My student driver and I walked to a gas station. A police car drove up and the officer informed the student in no uncertain terms that the car had to be moved off the road or it would be towed. I approached him cautiously, sensing his humorless mood.

"Excuse me," I said. "I'm speaking at the university tonight. Before the car is towed, I need to get my things out of the trunk."

"Get in the back of my car," he barked. "We'll drive over and wait for the tow truck."

As we sat in the snowstorm, I like a felon behind the metal grate separating the front seat from the back, the police officer broke the long silence by asking, "So, what are you talking about tonight?"

"Don't tell him," cautioned the wounded child within.

"Don't let him bully you," admonished my internal angry gay activist.

"Homophobia," I said with a forced smile.

"Oh yeah? That's the fear of homosexuals, isn't it?" he asked.

"Yes, it is," I replied, somewhat startled.

"Well, I got rid of that a long time ago. Our next-door neighbor was gay. He used to baby-sit me. My family was crazy about him. I called him Uncle Bob. He was a great guy," he said enthusiastically.

I have had similarly enlightened encounters with Army generals, coaches, cab drivers, elderly women and men, teenagers, and people of all races and religions. What I've learned is that my view of the world didn't work very well for me. My heterosexism, homophobia, and heterophobia made me miserable. I lived as a victim, isolated from and angrily reactive to others. I finally decided I didn't want to live like that anymore. It wasn't healthy and it wasn't fun.

It isn't easy to challenge old ways of thinking, but it's liberating. When the Born Again Christian Republican from Cobb County asked me if I was married and what I did for a living, I could have refused to talk to him. I could have dodged his question or I could have lectured him angrily. I'm glad I didn't.

A few years ago, I was asked to address the question "Are gay people part of God's plan?"

I answered that, when I die, I imagine God will say to me, as I imagine God will say to each of us, "Brian, did you sing the song I taught you?"

I said that I will respond, "God, for the first twenty-six years of my life I was too afraid. Instead I sang, 'I am Brian. I'm a heterosexual.' I feared that if I sang *my* song I'd lose everything—my family, my friends, my job. I feared that if I came out I would lose the love and respect of the important people in my life.

"But this voice inside me kept saying, 'That's not the song I taught you.'

"Then, feeling very alone, very frightened, hurt, angry, and defeated, I drank the turpentine and took all of the pills. I wanted to die. Like Martin Luther King, Jr., I wanted to be 'Free at last! Free at last!' But in a moment of grace I changed my mind.

"I had my stomach pumped and I began to sing, 'I am Brian. I am gay. Won't you accept me today?'

"I sang that song for many, many years as I traveled throughout North America telling my story and hoping that people would love me. I worked hard at being the best little gay boy in the world. Perhaps I would be okay, I thought, if I was just as—if not more—spiritual than heterosexuals, and just as—if not more—hardworking than heterosexuals, and just as—if not more—committed to my relationship, my family, civil rights, and so on, than heterosexuals. Then I would be acceptable, lovable, and respectable as a gay person.

"But the voice inside me kept saying, 'That's not the song I taught you.'

"I'm not sure exactly how it happened, maybe turning forty helped, but I finally found my song and I learned to sing it with confidence and pride.

"Today, I sing, 'I am Brian. I am gay. I'm God's gift to you today!' "

I *was* God's gift to the man on the plane. He needed to know intimately someone who was gay, and I enabled him to do so. Likewise, he was God's gift to me. My soul needed to know the soul of a Born Again Christian from Cobb County, Georgia.

I can be God's gift to each person I encounter, but only if I sing my song.

Our song is our story. People won't always accept the story as a gift, but not to sing our song is to condemn ourselves to deathly silence and to deny ourselves and others the opportunity of living life fully.

ABOUT
SEXUALITY

"SEX"

I wrote the word as big as I could on the giant sign I posted in my all-boys Catholic high school.

"Now that I have your undivided attention," it said, "vote Lion Party."

I was the sixteen-year-old, sexually naive, closeted campaign manager of a group seeking student council offices, and I'm sure I thought of myself as very daring.

In 1964, nice boys my age and of my religious and ethnic background didn't talk about sex in public, much less write the word in two-foot letters for all of the faculty to see. I recall excitedly watching from the sidelines as other sexually challenged male students elbowed each other with delight. I had spoken their secret language and had successfully gained their attention, their respect, and perhaps their vote.

Thirty-some years later, I self-consciously admit to urging my publisher to put the image of a "sexy" man and woman on the front cover of this book to gain the notice of gay, lesbian, and bisexual readers. "Now that I have *your* undivided attention, please buy my book."

I do so as an openly gay, mostly sexually satisfied, certified sexuality educator.

So why after all of these years am I aware of still feeling somewhat self-conscious and uncomfortable when I bring up the subject of sex to my gay peers? Why do I sometimes feel that even with them, I can be on the sidelines?

As a high school student who wanted to belong to the group, I knew that my homosexual feelings, if expressed, would prevent me from ever gaining status. Therefore, like most other gay or lesbian youths, I kept my mouth shut.

Now, as a gay man near fifty, finally liberated from the oppressive heterosexist confines of my adolescence, I painfully reflect that I've often continued to keep quiet about sexuality from fear of *losing* respect among some in the gay, lesbian, and bisexual communities.

For example, many years ago, during my first memorial service for a friend who had died of AIDS, a man stood and passionately pleaded with the mourners.

"Don't let this stop you from having glorious homo sex," he said. "Fucking had nothing to do with David's death. It's a government plot to stop us from giving and receiving pleasure. Fuck like bunnies!"

I was stunned. No one in Boston's Arlington Street Church said a thing in response. I was very angry at him for politicizing David's death in what I considered a terribly inappropriate manner. But I was also incredibly confused.

"What if he's right?" I worried, doubting what I had felt certain to be the truth about HIV transmission. "Are you sure that it's *not* a government effort to control gay men? Are you certain that unprotected anal sex with an infected person *is* responsible for David's death?" I asked myself.

Worse than the confusion I felt, though, was the *fear* I experienced at that moment. I'm embarrassed to admit that I was afraid of challenging this very vocal gay man because I thought it would impact my safe place in the gay community. I didn't want to risk losing status by being called an "uptight, sex-negative Uncle Tom" by him or anyone else.

Many times, before and since that incident, I've felt the same anger, confusion, and fear in response to other "gay sex" controversies, such as the place of the North American Man-Boy Love Association (NAMBLA) in the gay movement, the appropriateness of sanctioning sex clubs during the battle against AIDS, the value of confrontational erotic displays during pride marches, and the issue of sadomasochism in lesbian and gay lovemaking.

Sex can be a sacred cow for many people in the gay liberation movement, and I've found that discussing the subject with them can be an intimidating trip through a minefield. For some, there seems to be an unwritten rule that any questioning of another gay person's sexual attitudes or behaviors is oppressive to that person and treasonous to the movement. As a result, even when I've felt the need to talk through my uncertain feelings so that I could respond maturely to pressing public issues, I've more often than not tiptoed along the edge hoping to avoid an explosion. But I haven't done so proudly.

I understand and share the concern some people have about the destructive effect that moralizing can have on personal growth. Like most gay, lesbian, and bisexual people, I've taken refuge in the gay community from the harshly judgmental attitudes and punitive behaviors of the church and state with regard to homosexuality. In that safe space, I have matured emotionally through the encouragement and support I've received from the movement to freely explore and express my sexuality.

It has been a wonderful gift, and I don't want to give up any of that freedom. Nor do I want to make it less safe for other gay, lesbian, or bisexual people to explore and express their sexuality. That's why it can feel so uncomfortable offering a contrary or challenging position to other gay people about issues involving sexual health and values.

On the other hand, I've learned how important and helpful it is to talk through my uncertainties freely and openly and to express my insights about sexuality with small groups of friends. It broadens my knowledge, builds my confidence, and liberates me to be more intimate. That's why I'm eager to continue and expand the process. I believe that other gay people, and heterosexuals too, are interested in doing the same. But we can't do so standing timidly, quietly, and fearfully on the sidelines.

For many years, the gay movement has been mostly *reactive* to heterosexist concepts of sexual health and sexual values. We've withdrawn from mainstream societal institutions and have expended our considerable energy defending ourselves against charges of "deviance," "immaturity," "arrested development," "sexual obsession," and "pedophilia," among others. We have also valiantly railed against the excluding, demeaning ethic that values sexual behavior only as a means to procreation.

For the most part, we've needed to be so reactive in order just to survive. Many of us sense, though, that we're strong and confident enough today to be more *proactive* with regard to sexuality and to boldly explore how our unique experiences as homosexuals and bisexuals have impacted our concepts, our expression, and the development of our values. The time seems right for us to positively address some basic issues in our lives, and to see what common ground, if any, we share with heterosexuals.

To assist the discussion, I pose three basic questions:

1. What is *sexuality,* and is it the same for heterosexuals, homosexuals, and bisexuals?

2. What does it mean to be *sexually healthy,* and can gay people be so in a homophobic, heterosexist society? If so, what are the characteristics of sexually healthy gay, lesbian, and bisexual people?

3. In the absence of meaningful moral support and guidance from most societal institutions, including religions, are there *guidelines* that help gay people make life-enhancing, ethical decisions about their sexuality? If so, are those guidelines different for heterosexuals?

WHAT IS SEXUALITY?

If anyone had asked me, "What do you mean by 'SEX'?" when I spray-painted the word on the high school poster, I would have said something like, "Sex is when a guy puts his penis in a girl's vagina."

I knew, from personal experience, that one could also masturbate, but I wouldn't have trusted that that behavior fit in the category of "sex." Certainly the message that I received from those around me was that masturbation was "self-abuse" and a sign of immaturity that should not be talked about openly.

I also knew that I wanted to "sleep" with Robert Conrad, the virile television actor from the series *Hawaiian Eye* and *The Wild Wild West*—though I didn't know exactly what I was supposed to do sexually with him or have done to me—and I certainly wouldn't have been comfortable identifying that behavior as "sex" either.

No, *real* sex was what happened between a man and a woman in bed at night with the lights out.

The Sexuality Information and Education Council of the United States (SIECUS) offers a much broader definition.

"Human sexuality," they say, "encompasses the sexual knowledge, beliefs, attitudes, values, and behaviors of individuals. Its various dimensions include the anatomy, physiology, and biochemistry of the sexual response system; identity, orientation, roles, and personality; and thoughts, feelings, and relationships. The expression of sexuality is influenced by ethical, spiritual, cultural, and moral concerns."[1]

That's a lot more detailed than my earlier definition of sex as "a guy's penis in a girl's vagina." The more comprehensive description is a lot less focused on behavior, and it certainly better fits my gay experience of sexuality. It also builds an important bridge for discussions with heterosexuals.

Some people mistakenly believe that gay sexuality and straight sexuality are very different. Focusing solely on behavior, they imagine that the intensity of the sexual drive, the rationale for coming together, and the scope and frequency of sexual activities are what separates homosexuals from heterosexuals.

I believe that gay sexuality, bisexuality, and straight sexuality are basically the same. What separates us are not the components of our sexuality, nor the extent to which we are sexual, but rather the incentives, license, and opportunities we each have to explore, express, and grow into our sexuality.

Clearly, it's easier today to know, to claim, and to comfortably engage in one's sexuality if one is predetermined to be heterosexual than it is if one is born homosexual or bisexual. The church, state, and popular culture strongly encourage and reward heterosexual identity and expression.

Nevertheless, I was able to learn for myself that my sexuality is more about who I *am* than what I *do*. It's about my mind, body, and spirit experiencing themselves in harmony and at peace with the world. In that way, my sexuality is inseparable from my spirituality. What I do with my body for pleasure affects, consciously or unconsciously, the expansion of my mind and the direction of my soul's journey.

My sexuality is about how I express myself as a human being, celebrating and utilizing both my masculinity and my femininity, my weakness and my strength, my commonness and my uniqueness. It's about my openness to complete pleasure and my acceptance of complete responsibility for my thoughts, feelings, and behaviors.

In embracing my sexuality, I want nothing human to frighten, disgust, or alienate me from others or myself. At the same time, I want to acknowledge my ability to say "yes" or "no" and to accept that my decisions impact me and others.

As such, I suspect that I can experience myself in much the same way as most other humans do, regardless of their orientation. That is because the components of sexuality are the same for us all.

SEXUAL HEALTH

That said, is it possible to achieve sexual healthiness in a heterosexist, homophobic society? If so, how would sexually healthy gay, lesbian, or bisexual people behave?

Would they, for instance, need to be monogamous? Would they always disclose their HIV status to a potential sex partner? Would they ever have sex with a minor? Would they allow someone to inflict pain on them or would they do so themselves to others? Would they need to be in a primary relationship? Could they be celibate?

SIECUS recently compiled a long list of life behaviors of a sexually healthy adult. These include the ability to:

- appreciate one's own body
- interact with both genders in respectful and appropriate ways
- affirm one's own sexual orientation and respect the sexual orientation of others
- express love and intimacy in appropriate ways
- avoid exploitative or manipulative relationships

- exhibit skills that enhance personal relationships
- identify and live according to one's values
- communicate effectively with family, peers, and partners
- enjoy and express one's sexuality throughout life
- express one's sexuality in ways congruent with one's values
- engage in sexual relationships that are characterized by honesty, equity, and responsibility
- prevent sexual abuse
- avoid contracting or transmitting a sexually transmitted disease, including HIV
- demonstrate tolerance for people with different sexual values and lifestyles
- avoid behaviors that exhibit prejudice and bigotry
- educate others about sexuality

Clearly this abbreviated list represents the *ideal*—a status to strive toward. Few if any individuals can claim to live out all of these behaviors in a consistent manner.

Had I looked at this list in my early twenties, I would certainly have been confused and intimidated. How was I supposed to communicate effectively with family, peers, and partners? I was a skin-hungry, mixed-up, closeted gay kid who sneaked into bars in a desperate search for a same-sex partner, with whom I hoped to live happily ever after.

Even in my thirties, after I'd found a mate and started therapy, I would still have been embarrassed by the number of behaviors that I had not mastered. I sure didn't appreciate my body. And I certainly didn't always enjoy and express my sexuality. Nor did I always demonstrate tolerance for people with different sexual values and lifestyles. I drank too much, I was overly competitive with other gay men, and I resented like hell the social privileges of heterosexuals.

Today, in my late forties, I feel like I'm finally making some headway. At least I feel that I'm on the right track toward becoming a sexually healthy person. And yet . . . I still have lots of questions, doubts, concerns, and fears. Obviously, it's a lifelong trek, but one we need to make.

I believe that sexual healthiness is critical to life-enhancing decision making. This is true not just with regard to what we do with our bodies but also to our thoughts, feelings, and behaviors in all areas of our lives. What we know and feel about our own sexuality and that of others, and the freedom we have to express ourselves, affects every aspect of our being.

But there are enormous obstacles to becoming sexually healthy. Sexologists have identified sexual *ignorance, secrecy,* and *trauma* as the three major roadblocks to human beings maturing into their sexuality. All of us—gay, straight, and bisexual—confront the same basic obstacles, yet for many of us growing up gay, the challenges can be far more complex.

Consider the roadblocks.

IGNORANCE

"What's that?" the guy asks pointing at her breasts and vulva, in the whispered playground joke of my youth.

"These are my headlights and that's my grass," she says.

"And what's that?" she asks, pointing at his penis.

"That's my snake," he says.

Later, in bed, he awakens her: "Hey, turn on your headlights. My snake got lost in your grass."

Ha. Ha. I laughed along with the other pubescent boys, but I didn't completely understand. "What does he mean, *lost?*" Yet I pretended to know.

Clearly, I was sexually ignorant, not only in grade school, but also in high school and, believe it or not, through much of college. Like most people I know, gay and straight, I pretended to know about sex for fear of being discovered as "naive." But I had good reason to be sexually ignorant. There was no healthy discussion of sexuality in my home. Instead of being "pregnant," for instance, a woman was "in a family way."

As I recall, Mom didn't talk about sex at all. She didn't encourage questions or discussion, and she insisted upon complete modesty at all times.

I remember the first time I decided to sleep in the nude. I was no more than eleven. My nine-year-old brother, Tommy, watched from his twin bed as I pulled my underwear off beneath the sheets and dropped it to the floor.

"What are you doing?" he asked.

"I'm sleeping in the nude," I replied.

"That's a sin," he said.

"No it's not. Adam and Eve were nude," I answered confidently.

"Oh yeah," he said in recognition as he dropped his own underwear to the floor. Just then, Mom stepped into the doorway.

"Tommy, come here. I want to talk with you," she said.

"No, Mom, I'm tired," he pleaded.

"No, Tommy, come here. Right now," she persisted, knowing full well from her eavesdropping why he was so resistant.

"It's Brian's fault," he proclaimed from the bed. "He told me that Adam and Eve did it!"

My mother was a great mom but a horrible sex educator. I don't blame her, though. She too grew up sexually ignorant and secretive, and just passed on the multigenerational legacy to us.

It was apparently Dad's responsibility to teach us what we needed to know about sex. His "sex talk," however, was not at all helpful. Nor were the *Playboy* magazines he left in our room for Tommy and me to find.

In church and in Catholic grade school I did learn a lot about sexual *sins*. Under the Sixth Commandment category of *adultery,* they were referred to as "impure thoughts," "impure words," and "impure deeds." But no one supplied the details.

In four years of high school, I recall one presentation on sexuality. A teacher showed us a half-hour film from the Navy on gonorrhea. There was no discussion. Senior year, we were all required to attend a weekend retreat during which we got a "sex talk" from a doctor. I only remember him saying that if we were still masturbating, we were too immature to marry.

At Marquette University, every student had to take a course in Christian marriage in order to graduate. Each class day, the elderly Jesuit instructor would read aloud the chapter he had assigned as homework. The only chapter he didn't read aloud was the very bland one on heterosexual sex.

In the absence of accurate information presented in an appropriate manner, it's no wonder that I was sexually ignorant. I didn't understand much about my own body, or know anything about the bodies of females. I wasn't told about puberty, about intercourse, or about self-pleasuring.

I discovered masturbation quite by accident at about age fourteen. I was on my stomach, unconsciously rubbing up and down on my bed one night because it felt good. Suddenly there was an "explosion" that both scared the hell out of me and made me feel dizzy, giddy, and wonderful.

I feared that I had broken something—that a valve somewhere "down there" had been ruptured. I checked it out and realized that everything was intact but that I had made a sticky mess in the bed. "Yuck!" I cleaned it up as best and quietly as I could, so as not to draw Tommy's attention.

"What will Mom say?" I worried.

The next night, I repeated my activity from the evening before, but this time dared to imagine that I was in the arms of one of my male heroes from television. It was then that I first experienced the true meaning of "Wow!"

I also soon discovered that if I was quick enough, I could put my finger over the end of my penis before the "sticky stuff" came out, hold it, and when no one was looking, walk to the bathroom and let it flow into the toilet. No more telltale muss, except spiritually, because now my impure *thoughts* had turned into impure *deeds*.

Though my Irish Catholic background may appear remarkably repressed, my guess is that gay men and lesbians who grew up in sexually healthier environments still ended up sexually ignorant. Their parents, teachers, and counselors, like mine, assumed that they were heterosexual and provided information accordingly.

I have met no gay men or lesbian women whose parents prepared them for mature decision making around same-sex dating, much less discussed fellatio, cunnilingus, or anal sex. The story of the birds and the bees usually ended with the creation of other little birds and pollinated flowers.

Even today, most high school sexuality education programs are void of any positive mention of homosexuality. The materials are designed for pregnancy prevention and avoidance of sexually transmitted diseases. Like my generation before them, gay, lesbian, and bisexual youth are expected to learn the important facts about their sexuality on their own. Tragically, many of them are learning through experimentation, exposing themselves to life-threatening risks because they know no better.

SECRECY

Though I was very curious about sex, I was also frightened of it because it was generally considered morally bad and I wanted to be God's best friend.

I aspired to be a saint and learned from stories told reverently by the nuns about perfect people who shunned impure thoughts and deeds at all costs for the sake of their souls. Others who had wanted to be God's best friend, they said, had thrown themselves into thornbushes rather than think bad thoughts, and allowed themselves to be killed rather than engage in sinful deeds.

The shame brought on by my sexual feelings for Tarzan and my sexual rubbing in bed led me, therefore, to become extremely *secretive*. No one could ever know what bad things I was feeling or what sinful things I was doing. Even if I had wanted to talk to someone about my "Wow!" experiences in bed, I didn't have adequate language. I never quite connected all the jokes about "beating off" with what I did. What did you "beat"? If it hadn't been so unsettling, it would have been funny.

I recall that during my sophomore year in college, two fraternity brothers, with whom I shared a room, and I were lying in our beds, talking in the dark about masturbation.

"Ninety-nine percent of men masturbate," I said with great authority, attempting to make a case for its normalcy.

"Brian, that can't be true," protested the West Virginian we called Big Daddy. "More than one percent of the population don't have hands."

"Hands!" I thought. "What do *hands* have to do with it?" Though very confused, I knew better than to open my mouth.

In this area, my life was probably not unlike that of most homosexual and heterosexual youths who grew up at the same time as I. Certainly, the degree of ignorance and secretiveness one experienced was impacted by one's religion, ethnicity, and race, among other factors. Most people did not grow up wanting to be a saint. But most also didn't grow up thinking it was possible for them to acknowledge sexual feelings, or to ask sexual questions.

The degree of secrecy we maintained was also heavily impacted by our sexual orientation.

What separates gay people from straight people who are also attempting to climb out of this quagmire of sexual ignorance and secrecy is the availability of information about heterosexuality through television, movies, songs, books, jokes, and party gossip, and the public sanctioning of heterosexual feelings and behavior (especially for males). Gay, lesbian, and bisexual kids, on the other hand, grow up with no rungs on the ladder and encounter shoves rather than pulls from people at the top of the pit.

In a world in which your feelings are typically described as "sinful," "disgusting," "unnatural," "an abomination," and a sign of "mental illness," and would, if revealed, result in your being disowned, ostracized, bullied, condemned, and perhaps killed, you are not inclined to tell anyone what you are feeling or doing.

TRAUMA

In addition to a lack of accurate information and openness, some of us, gay and straight alike, also had bad sexual experiences as children that confused us and left us in varying degrees of trauma. Sexual abuse of children is very common in the United States, with one million children a year reportedly being touched inappropriately by an older child or an adult. Add to these the children who are emotionally scarred by the inappropriate seductive talk or behavior of an adult and the numbers are staggering.

In addition, most gay people have been enormously, if not consciously, traumatized by the social pressure they felt to identify and behave as a heterosexual, even though such pressure is not classified as sexual abuse by experts in the field.

Imagine how today's society would respond if heterosexual thirteen- to nineteen-year-olds were forced to date someone of the same sex. What would the reaction be if they were expected to hold the hand of, slow dance with, hug, kiss and say "I love you" to someone to whom they were not and could not be sexually attracted?

The public would be outraged! Adult supervisors would be sent to prison. Youthful "perpetrators" would be expelled from school. Years of therapy would be prescribed for the innocent victims of such abuse. Volumes would be written about the long-term effect of such abhorrent socialization (as today we lament the ill-conceived efforts to turn left-handed people into right-handed ones).

Yet, that's part of the everyday life of gay teenagers. And there's no comparable public concern, much less outcry, about the traumatizing effects on *their* sexuality.

Such ignorance, secrecy, and trauma enormously impact the journey of gay, lesbian, and bisexual people to sexual healthiness.

Regrettably, many of us, like our heterosexual sisters and brothers, continue to be sexually ignorant. Though we assume we're sophisticated about sexuality because we've performed sexually, we are often uninformed, anxious about what we don't know, and frustrated by the limits imposed by our lack of knowledge.

Gay, lesbian, and bisexual adults often also remain secretive about sexuality. Though we may joke incessantly about whose "legs are up in the air," we rarely talk to each other in a safe, non-judging, and open way about our feelings of inadequacy, our fears, our ignorance, or even our turn-ons.

Nor do we often talk with each other or with a trained counselor about the effects of the traumatizing sexual experiences we had either as adults or as children. We often fail to realize that the anger and shame that we carry within us as a result of those experiences enormously impact our ability to fully express and experience our sexuality in a healthy way.

How do people who are ignorant about sexuality, secretive about their "shameful" feelings and behaviors, and traumatized by childhood sexual experiences make mature decisions about their emotional and physical needs and boundaries? How do sexual adolescents, regardless of their age, make healthy decisions about whether, when, and under what circumstances to be sexual? How do they communicate their desires and limits? And how do sexually and emotionally hungry individuals, without benefit of accurate information or support, understand and respect the boundaries of others?

Human beings—gay, lesbian, bisexual, and straight—all come from the same primordial pool, and all struggle to survive and to evolve. We are intimately linked to each other by the experience of bodies, minds, and spirits hungering for sustenance. We're separated from one another in our search for personal and social harmony only by the force of our genetic influences and our social conditioning.

The characteristics of a sexually healthy person are the same for everyone, although circumstances can influence the ease with which one achieves sexual health. Gay people face particular challenges, given our minority status in a heterosexually defined culture. On the other hand, we are also freed from convention to explore the authentic nature of our sexuality.

As "sexual outlaws," to use author John Rechy's phrase,[2] we've had to make up the rules as we went along. The concepts of "marriage" and "family" needed to be redefined so as to be useful. With everything about us prohibited and punished by the church and state, we either shriveled up and died or we moved forward and lived outside of the law and social approval.

SEXUAL VALUES

If we chose to live, necessity prompted the creation of concepts, rituals, and values that were tailored to meet our particular needs. Many of us sought relationships free of roles, conceived of gender as free of boundaries, defined "fidelity" as emotional rather than necessarily genital, and perceived fantasies as tools to understand and tap the erotic nature of our souls.

In the process of this sexual search, we often found kindred spirits among heterosexuals who were also working to free themselves from concepts that did not meet their needs. Sexual healthiness is not defined by orientation. Nor are sexual values.

As SIECUS suggests, the sexually healthy person will "identify and live according to one's values . . . express one's sexuality in ways congruent with one's values."

As sexually healthy gay, lesbian, and bisexual people consider options for themselves—such as whether to have an open or closed relationship, or to engage in a new sexual activity—they employ guidelines that both reflect their experiences and are useful in evaluating the possibilities.

As gay people discuss among ourselves, and with the larger population of heterosexuals, important social issues such as effective HIV-prevention education and the repeal of sodomy laws, we look for a common language of concern. Agreement on what makes sexuality life-enhancing, not only for the individual but also for society, helps eliminate the us-versus-them mentality that so often sabotages meaningful conversation.

What values do sexually healthy homosexuals, bisexuals, and heterosexuals share?

Some time ago, I came across a presentation of sexual values that I found quite useful. Admittedly, I was initially very suspicious of them because they came from a group of Catholic theologians. "What do *they* have to say," I wondered, "that could be relevant to me?" Yet, I was delightfully surprised.

Their work never received an endorsement from the Church's hierarchy, but the writings of this Committee on Sexuality of the Catholic Theological Society of America, I feel, merits attention, if not appreciation. These men and women, lay and religious, married and celibate, took bold steps in 1977 to be inclusive in their visionary approach to sexuality, and they have provided us with a reasonable starting point for a discussion of shared values.

Human Sexuality, New Directions in American Catholic Thought, said the following:

> Human sexuality is the concrete manifestation of the divine call to completion, a call extended to every person in the very act of creation and rooted in the very core of his or her being.

From the first moment of existence it summons us incessantly to both intrapersonal and interpersonal growth. Intrapersonally, it propels each person toward the task of creating the male or female each was destined to be. Interpersonally, it calls each to reach out to the other without whom full integration can never be achieved. Thus, sexuality, like every other aspect of humanness, is destined to serve human relationships, not subjugate them. Sexuality is not just an isolated biological or physical phenomenon accidental to human beings but an integral part of their personal self-expression and of their mission of self-communication to others. . . .

In short, we maintain that it is appropriate to ask whether specific sexual behavior realizes certain values that are conducive to growth and integration of the human person. Among these values we would single out the following as particularly significant:

Self-liberating, other-enriching, honest, faithful, socially-responsible, life-serving, and joyous.[3]

What I like most about these descriptive words is how "user friendly" they are. Rather than exclude people by valuing sexual behavior solely for its procreative potential, these inclusive concepts build bridges of mutual respect to all sexual beings. They do so by emphasizing the positive results of healthy sexual expression.

I know that my sexual relationship with Ray can be as self-liberating, other-enriching, honest, faithful, socially responsible, life-serving, and joyous as that of any heterosexual couple, with or without children. So too can be my sexual relationship with myself.

Rather than focusing almost entirely on the *intent* of the behavior, these guidelines speak to us of the *impact* of our decisions. Thus they are equally applicable to people of all sexual orientations.

Had these words been used to frame our whole society's guidelines, we wouldn't today have sodomy laws that regulate the behaviors of homosexuals but not of heterosexuals. Nor would we need to debate the wisdom of promoting condoms to save people's lives during the HIV crisis. And had these words represented the official sexual values of the Vatican, I would have had no need to leave my Church in search of guidelines that were relevant to my life.

How are these words relevant to my sexual decision making?

When hearing a gay person implore others to "fuck like bunnies" during the AIDS epidemic, I have a language that helps me evaluate the behaviors. I can ask, for instance, whether it would be *socially responsible* for me to have unsafe, indiscriminate sex or to encourage others to do so?

If an adult talks of his or her desire to have sex with a minor, I can question whether it is an *enriching* experience for the youngster. Is the minor's consent informed, and free of other considerations, such as the need to survive? In other words, would it be *honest* behavior for the adult—or for me, were I so inclined?

As I learn of and reflect upon sexual behaviors that stretch my boundaries, I can ask myself if such practices would be *life-serving* or truly *joyous* for me. For instance, would those activities that often require drugs to block physical pain satisfy these criteria?

When young gay people ask about the appropriateness of an open relationship, I can help them evaluate their decisions by reviewing what conditions would allow them to find casual sex outside of a primary relationship to be *honest* and *faithful.*

I don't have the answer as to what is *honest* and *faithful* for others, nor do I know whether these and the other words provide a reliable guide for their sexual decision making. But I do generally trust these words as guides for me, even acknowledging that my values continue to evolve as I continue to get emotionally healthier.

My values come from my experiences, and I trust the insights that come from those experiences. They also come from listening to and reflecting upon the experiences of others, gay, straight, and bisexual.

The truth of our lives is in the paths we've walked and in the lessons we've learned. Our struggles for authentic living have made us wise, though sometimes we're not in touch with our gifts.

Our wisdom flows forth when we talk to one another and listen to one another with openness, vulnerability, trust, respect, and love about what we've seen, what we've done, where we are, and where we want to be. It is in such a space and time that the values of our lives emerge.

What words, then, if not these, describe the truth of our experiences? May I suggest a way to discern?

Ask a friend or two, gay or straight, to explore the topic of sexuality. Create an environment that feels safe and nonjudgmental. Then, together, ask each other these questions:

"What does 'sexuality' mean to you?"

"How would you describe a 'sexually healthy' person?"

"What values do you bring to sexual decision making?"

Other questions that are useful in surfacing insights with friends and lovers include:

"What messages did you get about sex when you were a child? How did you learn about sex?"

"When did you first realize that you were sexual? How did you feel about it?"

"How do you feel about your body? What do you like most about it? What least?"

"What goals do you have for yourself as a sexual person? How do you imagine they're different than the goals of others?"

Such open and loving discussions, beyond building strong relationships, go a long way in challenging the effects of sexual ignorance, secrecy, and trauma. They expand our understanding and appreciation of the full spectrum of human sexuality. They enable us to discern the values we employ for decision making, and they give us a language to address the issues which confront us in our daily lives. In other words, such efforts at intimacy engender increased sexual healthiness.

I find that most people, gay and straight, are eager to talk honestly about their sexuality, but they often feel awkward doing so because they've never before been given permission.

If you're so inclined but don't know how to get such a wonderful and important discussion started, I have another suggestion.

Simply say to a friend, "Can we talk about sex?"

If that doesn't work, try writing the word "SEX" in two-foot letters on a piece of construction board. Hang it on your front door, behind your work area, or in the back window of your car.

I guarantee a discussion will follow.

ABOUT
LOVE AND MARRIAGE

On the inside front page of my New American Bible, directly across from a head shot of an unsmiling Pope John Paul II, there appears "The Family Register."

When I was given the bible in 1986, as a thank-you for being godfather at my nephew Matthew's christening, I filled in the blanks in the area designated "Certificate of Marriage."

THIS CERTIFIES THAT *Brian McNaught* AND *Ray Struble* WERE UNITED IN HOLY MATRIMONY *Union* ON THE *4th* DAY OF *May* IN THE YEAR OF OUR LORD NINETEEN HUNDRED AND *76* AT *their apartment at 1035 Beacon Street, Brookline, Massachusetts,* BY *Mutual Consent and Affirmation.* WITNESS *Their friends, family &* *God* (though none but the last was present).

. . .

Ray and I have never had a commitment service to formalize our relationship. On our tenth anniversary, we did gather a small group of close friends for the first "official" celebration of our life together. On our twentieth, we had our picture taken so that people who care about us might always be reminded of the love we share.

We don't wear wedding rings, partly because I'm not partial to jewelry. Given our cultural background and perhaps our age, we're not inclined to hold hands in public. Yet, I imagine that even the most casual observers are aware that we're a couple. The deep care that we have for each other and the easy familiarity we feel comes through in a variety of subtle manners, such as in the way we taste each other's entrée at restaurants, share one drink and one popcorn at the movies, and critique each other's selections in the clothing store's dressing room.

"Nope. It makes you look fat."

Though we don't generally look lovingly into each other's eyes in public, what gives us away as lovers is probably how we encourage discussion of each other's accomplishments and tease about each other's idiosyncrasies. My guess is that people notice that we generally go into and out of the water at the same time, run in near-identical outfits at the same pace in the park, and stop in our tracks with a look of great concern if the other seems to be in difficulty or is out of sight.

"Where did you go? I'm going to get you one of those retractable leashes. You stay with me."

Ray is my best friend, as I am his. We each hurry home from the office or a road trip in excited anticipation of seeing the other. We both trust the other will enthusiastically celebrate with us the highlights of our day and sympathetically respond to the low points. Once together, we each feel safe, secure, and centered.

We're also soul mates. From our breakfast discussions at 5:30 before Ray leaves for the office to our whispered conversations as we snuggle in bed at 9:00, we chart and navigate together our spiritual journeys. We find in each other the encouragement to be honest with ourselves, to be true to what we know is right, and to accept ourselves as worthy of love and respect.

As a couple, Ray and I have created a third entity with a life and identity of its own. That entity is our loving relationship. Should either of us die, the entity would live. Likewise, though we both may continue to live, we know the relationship could die. That's why we work so hard to keep it alive.

Poets, artists, musicians, and other lovers throughout the ages have described much better than I can the nature of this love. The words of Ruth to Naomi in the Old Testament, for instance, help capture the spirit of our bond.

"Do not ask me to abandon or forsake you," she said, "for wherever you will go I will go, wherever you will lodge I will lodge, your people shall be my people, and your God my God. Wherever you will die I will die, and there be buried."[1]

This is all to suggest that the substance of the current emotional, national debate generated by the anticipated final ruling of the Hawaiian Supreme Court[2] supporting the right of gay and lesbian people to marry, and the reactionary so-called Defense of Marriage Act (DOMA)[3] doesn't reflect Ray's and my experience. For us, the issue is not about weddings in churches, "special rights," or being valued by society as equal to heterosexuals, as many radio talk show callers and many legislators insist. Nor is the issue about having the public legitimize that we are a couple or that we love one another. We already know that.

For us, the real issue of the Aloha State's saying that we can legally marry is that we might one day soon be free of the penalties imposed by our own state and the federal government for loving each other.

If one day we fly to Hawaii to get married, as I assume we will, it won't be to wear tuxedos or to get our names and picture in the paper. Like other gay and lesbian couples we know, we want to be left alone by the church and state. But we also want to be free from discrimination in our daily lives, and we want to avoid a nightmare of unfair battles with blood relatives, the state, and the IRS when one of us is sick or dies.

According to the Lambda Legal Defense and Education Fund, one of two lesbian and gay nonprofit legal organizations spearheading the campaign on this critically important marriage issue, there are a significant number of legal rights conferred by the state to heterosexual married couples but denied to gay and lesbian couples. These include:

- status as next of kin for hospital visits and medical decisions where one partner is too ill to be competent
- joint insurance policies for home, auto, and health
- joint parenting; joint adoption; joint foster care, custody and visitation
- automatic inheritance in the absence of a will
- inheritance of jointly owned real and personal property through the right of survivorship
- benefits such as annuities, pension plans, Social Security, and Medicare
- dissolution and divorce protections such as community property and child support
- immigration and residency for partners from other countries
- joint leases with automatic renewal rights in the event one partner dies or leaves the house or apartment
- spousal exemptions to property tax increases upon the death of one partner who is a co-owner of the home
- veteran's discounts on medical care, education, and home loans
- joint filing of tax returns; joint filing of customs claims when traveling
- wrongful death benefits for a surviving partner and children

- bereavement or sick leave to care for a partner or child
- decision-making power with respect to whether a deceased partner will be cremated or not and where to bury him or her
- domestic violence protection orders
- crime victim's recovery benefits

My guess is that most gay, lesbian, and bisexual people are unaware of all that homosexual couples are legally denied. I know this is true of heterosexuals. (Until recently, many straight people were unaware that gay people *couldn't* marry.) I certainly had no idea of how difficult the state has made it for committed gay relationships.

When Ray and I came together as "roommates" in 1976, we divided the rent, checked off our calls from the telephone bill, and carefully recorded what we each were spending on groceries, flowers, and magazine subscriptions, among other items.

A year later, when it was clear to us that we were in a primary relationship that we both wanted to last forever, we merged our meager bank accounts and abandoned our itemized lists. Wanting to be very responsible about financial matters though, we also signed papers that said if one of us died, the other would inherit everything, and that if we broke up, we would split everything fifty-fifty.

It didn't matter to either of us who made more money. In the beginning, neither of us made much. Ray spent his days as an entry-level employee at an investment firm and his nights as a student working to get his college degree. I worked out of the apartment, writing a column in the gay press, editing two community newspapers, and speaking to whoever would pay my transportation costs. I also managed our affairs, ensuring, for instance, that Ray's dinner was ready so that he could eat before rushing off to class.

Life was pretty simple when we were in our late twenties. What we needed, we bought together. And we didn't need much.

When we came together, I had a car, a dog, plants, and knick-knacks. Ray had furniture. What more could we want?

It was irrelevant who pulled out the cash for a movie or the credit card for dinner. It all came out of the same account. We made enough money on which to live. We wanted for nothing and we loved each other completely.

As we got a little older, things became a little more complicated. In our thirties, as usually happens, we both started making more money. For us, that meant we started thinking about buying things, like a newer car, more furniture, and more knick-knacks. We eventually even made enough to buy a little cabin on a remote lake. Ray was earning more than I, so we decided to put the cabin in his name for tax purposes. But that didn't bother me, because I knew it was my cabin too. Or so I assumed.

When I started working for the mayor of Boston in the spring of 1982, our two incomes enabled us to buy a home. With both names on the mortgage, our life again became more complicated. Who would take the deduction on his income tax?

"How does it work for heterosexuals who are married?" I asked.

"It doesn't matter how it works for heterosexuals," I was told by an attorney friend. "The state doesn't recognize your relationship to Ray."

Amazingly, I hadn't thought about it much before, but I remember suddenly feeling very resentful. Until we needed to make important financial decisions, the position of the state or the church on my relationship with Ray didn't affect me. I didn't want or need a marriage license or the church's blessing to legitimize my love for him. Yet, I didn't want to have to finagle legal remedies to tax situations either (an expensive problem my married heterosexual siblings don't face).

Our lives were complicated further as we became more successful and as we began addressing the issues of health care and retirement. We were advised by other gay friends to have living wills drawn up and to name each other as the decision maker in life-and-death situations. In the absence of a marriage license, we were warned, the state would consider us single and look for guidance from blood relations.

We also decided to increase our life insurance policies to do more than just cover the costs of funerals, given the hefty inheritance tax we would face when one of us died. Finally, we started individual retirement accounts (IRAs) and named each other as beneficiary.

By our forties, Ray was making considerably more money than I. We had bought a second car and upgraded the quality of our furniture and accessories. Improvements on the house and the cottage required larger mortgages. Insurance policies were purchased to cover the cost of the mortgage in the event that one of us died. Still, we had but one bank account.

Because of the AIDS epidemic, we became even more aware of how insignificant our relationship was in the eyes of the state. As the mayor's ombudsperson to the gay community, I was often asked to help men get access to their lovers in hospital intensive care units. If you weren't married or related by blood, hospital regulations prohibited such visitation. Funeral directors could ignore the requests of the surviving partner, and landlords could evict him or her. Estranged parents could clean out all of their son's personal possessions with the blessing of the courts. If there were any questions as to who owned what, they could take those items too. None of this would be possible if a gay couple's relationship had any legal status.

Ray and I also picked up from conversations with some family members the assumption that if one of us died, his wealth would go not to the survivor but to the family, as if we were merely roommates who had shared expenses for twenty years. Though we got assurances from our gay younger brothers that they would never allow such a thing to happen, we nevertheless became more concerned about our legal rights.

We might have felt incapable of navigating the legal minefield gay couples inhabit were it not for our friend Carl. He was an extraordinarily bright attorney, a former judge, and a state cabinet member under two administrations. Before he came out, there had been considerable talk about his prospects of becoming governor. He was fiscally conservative and a stickler for detail.

Carl took one look at our simple wills and other legal documents, rolled his eyes, and encouraged us to allow his very prestigious law firm to draw up ironclad documents that would protect us from the state and from our families. Several thousand dollars later, we had very sophisticated wills and documents that were guaranteed to ensure we would be treated equal to surviving heterosexual marriage partners.

Among the special provisions was one that bequeathed the majority of Ray's estate to a charitable trust. Upon his death, named executors would disperse to me a yearly sum as deemed adequate to meet my needs. Upon my death, that portion of the estate would go to designated charities.

As the one who wrote the majority of the checks from the joint account for gas, electric, donations, subscriptions, and groceries, I wasn't used to thinking in terms of "Ray's estate" and "Brian's estate." When I made deposits at the bank, my payroll checks and his were submitted together. He made more money, but we always thought of it as *our* money. However, the state doesn't.

It also didn't sit well with me that someone else would be given authority to decide how much of the estate I needed in order to live. My father didn't have that happen when my mother died, nor would my mother have suffered such indignity had my father preceded her. (And she hadn't added a dollar to their savings from work outside the home.)

I soon found myself becoming self-conscious about what was *Ray's* and what was *mine;* about his income and mine; about which documents, such as car titles, carried his name and which carried mine. Even trusting that he loved me completely and would honor our agreement about splitting everything fifty-fifty, I was aware of questioning how I would live if I lost the financially secure future and lifestyle his better income provided.

Thus I found that, rather than having no impact on our lives as a gay couple as I had once imagined, the state's discriminatory treatment of our relationship was destructive to the harmony of my life with Ray. But as annoying as the state's laws and society's attitudes were, we had a clever, highly respected, well-connected gay attorney who, because of our ability to pay for an elaborate set of documents, was able to maneuver us through the mess and allow us to spend our time and energy on building the relationship.

When Carl (a pseudonym I know he would appreciate) died of AIDS at age sixty-five, his memorial service was attended by the chief justice of the state supreme court, the family of one former governor whom he'd served, and politicians, attorneys, and other state luminaries, as well as gay friends and family members. After several impressive testimonies, Carl was eulogized by his lover of twenty-three years, our dear friend John. John spoke eloquently and with dignity of their life together and played to the hushed and deeply moved gathering a recording of a beautiful duet by two men from Bizet's opera *The Pearl Fishers*.

It was all lovely, and, to the casual eye, a fine celebration of the life and love of an admired gay man. Yet, for John, I later learned, it was a brave front to the chaos surrounding the death of his gay spouse.

"Carl was specific that he wanted to be cremated," John told me, "but the funeral home insisted upon receiving the permission of a blood relative."

"Didn't you have power of attorney?" I asked incredulously.

"That ends when the person dies," he explained. "I was just

lucky Carl had a niece in California who was willing to fax her consent. I don't know what I would have done."

Carl and John had purchased side-by-side plots in the village cemetery but hadn't arranged in advance for cremation. Even if Carl had, his wishes could have been contested by a blood relative, and John, again, would have had no legal right to intercede. Had they been a heterosexual couple, it wouldn't have been an issue.

"I made all of the arrangements, wrote the obit, worked with the funeral home and the church, but I never felt I was in good legal standing," John said. "I knew I had influential contacts should I need them, but I thought 'Pity the poor souls who don't.' "

When John went to change the utilities over to his name, he was informed that the telephone company and others would have to treat him as a new account, conduct a check on his credit history, and require a deposit. This solely because it was Carl, not he, who had made the initial call to set up the account, though it was John who had written the payment checks for twenty-three years.

Carl's IRAs named John as beneficiary, but John was informed that he couldn't roll over the IRAs into his own IRA account as a surviving heterosexual spouse could do. Instead, he would have to sell Carl's IRAs and pay taxes on them, and then he would be free to invest what money remained.

The most horrifying time for John came when Carl's estate needed to be appraised. In Carl's absence, John took comfort in the sight of the chair his lover most often sat in for reading, the paintings that they bought together on vacation, the porcelain bowl they purchased as a memorial when their beloved golden retriever died.

"But, who owns what?" he was asked, so that the state could assess Carl's possessions.

"We never kept receipts," John told me. "Everything was *ours*. Our lives were so meshed. Yet, they were saying, 'You're not a

couple. You're *individuals*. It's not joint. You have to divide it up.'
I had to say, 'This was his. This is mine. He gave me that ten years
ago.' It was awful."

On the wall was a large painting of a rocking horse. The well-
known Santa Fe artist was a friend of Carl's. "I remember when
he bought that for me in 1982. The artist had left an open heart
on the painting and Carl had him write 'Gio' in it," John said.
("Gio" was Carl's pet name for his lover, short for the Italian
translation of John, Giovanni.)

"Heterosexual partners wouldn't have to go through all of
that upon the death of their loved one," he said. "It's so unfair."

Equally unfair was the way John has been treated by Carl's law
partners. One of them, for instance, brought into the firm by Carl
and entertained in his home, not only did not attend Carl's
memorial service but never expressed either in writing or verbally
his condolences to John.

While the Hawaiian Supreme Court ruling won't legislate
common courtesy, a change in the law regarding the status of
gay unions may one day impact the public's response to gay and
lesbian survivors.

It is hard for John to understand how most straight people,
and even some gay ones, respond to his loss. "It would be very
different," he said, "if I were a heterosexual widower."

Even many straight people who knew and loved them both
as a couple haven't been able to reach out. "I don't think they
know what to say, so they act as if it didn't happen," John explained. "I have gotten the best support from straight men and
women who have lost their spouses. They understand and can
talk about the huge void that is left in your life."

Remarkably, many of John's gay friends don't bring up Carl's
name either. "I censor myself because I think people don't want
to hear it, perhaps because they have been faced with so much
loss already," John told me. "Some people, on the other hand,
act as if I just lost a pet, as if I should go out and get another one
soon."

Most fair-minded people would be horrified that John has been faced with such state-sanctioned hostility and insensitivity in response to his loss. Yet it goes on every day in the lives of gay and lesbian people throughout the country. Until recently, we have simply endured the humiliation, frustration, and anger we felt, and have coped the best we could. Some of us have sought to protect ourselves by maneuvering through small openings in the legal system. But John's troubles, particularly given Carl's sophisticated knowledge of the law and his prestigious social standing, have made Ray and me much less confident about how well protected we now are.

Again, that is why the anticipated Hawaiian Supreme Court ruling, DOMA, and the battles that now rage in state legislatures around the country are so important to us.

According to Evan Wolfson, the bright young director of the Marriage Project at Lambda who is feverishly attempting to coordinate the direction of this legal debate, we can take some comfort in the historic precedents to this case.

At one time, black people living in this country were forbidden to marry each other. Their loving unions had no status. Later, black Americans were prohibited from marrying white people. The same was true for Asians. One judge wrote: "Almighty God created the races white, black, yellow, malay and red, and he placed them on separate continents. And but for the interference with his arrangement there would be no cause for such marriages. The fact that he separated the races shows that he did not intend for the races to mix."[4]

In 1925, a San Diego judge wrote: "The dominant race of the country has a perfect right to exclude other races from equal rights with its own people."[5]

As syndicated columnist Deb Price aptly notes, the current debate is about whether "the dominant sexual orientation of the country has a perfect right to exclude the gay minority from equal access to marriage."[6]

Now that it seems likely Hawaii's Supreme Court will uphold

the ruling that gay and lesbian people can marry in that state, and thus be entitled to the same legal protections afforded to heterosexuals married there, the question of the hour is whether the other forty-nine states will ultimately recognize, by choice or force, the validity of the marriage.

If Ray and I flew to Hawaii to be married legally, just as heterosexuals are free to do in any state, could we then file joint IRS tax returns? How about joint California state tax returns? Will a Massachusetts funeral director abide by our wishes? If we adopt, does the child have two legal parents wherever our family travels or only when we are in Hawaii? When one of us dies, is the inheritance going to be outrageously taxed or, one day, will our home state be required to recognize that it was our joint income?

If Utah recognizes the legitimacy of the marriage vows made by a heterosexual couple at the top of a roller coaster in Ohio or while bungee jumping in Florida, can they get away with not recognizing the marriage certificate issued by the state of Hawaii to their gay and lesbian tax-paying Utah citizens?

Wolfson at Lambda, and the dozens of attorneys at other organizations working on behalf of gay civil rights, argue that Utah and those other states that take such a stand do so illegally, despite guidance from Congress to the contrary. They cite as the most persuasive reason for this the "full faith and credit" clause of the U.S. Constitution (Article 4), which states:

> Full Faith and Credit shall be given in each State to the public Acts, Records, and judicial Proceedings of every other State. And the Congress may by general laws prescribe the manner in which such Acts, Records and Proceedings shall be proved and the Effect thereof.

In legal briefs on the subject, Lambda also notes the "Uniform Marriage and Divorce Act," signed by seventeen states (including Utah), which says:

All marriages contracted within this State prior to the effective date of the ACT, or outside this State, that were valid at the time of the contract or subsequently validated by the laws of the place in which they were contracted or by the domicile of the parties, are valid in this State.

Writing about the Defense of Marriage Act, Wolfson refers to "DOMA's blatant violation of constitutional principles of federalism, nondiscrimination and respect for lawful marriages," and he states: "Once we win the freedom to marry, we will challenge this sweeping and invidious federal discrimination as couples fight to protect their families and their lawful marriages, state by state, court by court."[7]

Ultimately, the U.S. Supreme Court will decide on the full implications of the Hawaiian court ruling and on the constitutionality of DOMA. But it will be a long, hard battle before the legal status of gay unions is recognized in all fifty states and by the federal government. Patience, perseverance, hard work, and a positive attitude will be required of everyone.

Some people may be shocked to learn that it was as recently as 1967 that sixteen states prohibited marriage between a black person and a white person (miscegenation). Virginia law, for instance, stated:

All marriages between a white person and a colored person shall be absolutely void without any decree of divorce or other legal process."[8]

Shortly after they were married in 1958, Mildred Jeter Loving, who was black, and her white husband, Richard Loving, were arrested as felons for violating Virginia's law. They faced up to five years in prison. Instead, the trial judge forbade them from setting foot in their home state for twenty-five years.

Finally, in 1967 the U.S. Supreme Court ruled in *Loving v. Virginia* that all state marriage laws containing "same-race restrictions" were unconstitutional. It said:

The freedom to marry has long been recognized as one of the vital personal rights essential to the orderly pursuit of happiness by free men.

Yet, it may not follow that the Supreme Court will immediately rule as unconstitutional the "same-sex restrictions" in state and federal marriage laws.

It's important to remember that simply flying to Hawaii to get married won't protect lesbian and gay couples from punitive actions by the other states or by the U.S. government. I recommend, therefore, a three-pronged approach for all gay, lesbian, and bisexual people who have been, are now, or want to be in a committed loving relationship:

1. Work like hell in your own state to educate others about the issue.

2. Protect yourselves today from discrimination by employing every legal option currently available.

3. Don't lose focus of the bottom line: no law passed or rescinded can diminish the integrity, beauty, or goodness of a lesbian or gay male love relationship.

As the "gays in the military" debate made clear, we can't assume our national gay civil rights organizations can completely manage important community issues. Nor can we count on the good will of well-intentioned politicians. Each gay, lesbian, and bisexual person needs to be involved in any way he or she can.

Our goal is to impact public opinion and legislation. This can entail:

• Learning the facts. To do so, we can contact Lambda, the American Civil Liberties Union, the Gay and Lesbian Advocates and Defenders (GLAD), or some other legal resource (see Resources, "Legal").

• Making allies. We need to talk about the issue with gay and straight family members, friends, and colleagues. We need to ask our professional and social associations to take a stand. We can write letters to the editor, call in to radio talk shows, wear buttons, and display bumper stickers. If the public supports legal protections for gay unions, legislators are less likely to pass discriminatory bills.

• Lobbying. If our state introduces an anti-marriage bill, we need to meet with our state representative and senator. Bring them literature. Write them letters. And we should do the same with our city legislators. Many of them don't have a face to put with the issue.

• Volunteering our services to national or local organizations and coalitions that are working on the issue.

• Donating money to support the legal and educational efforts that are being made.

Ray and I know that for the foreseeable future we can't count on an anticipated marriage certificate from the state of Hawaii to protect us in couple-related legal issues at home. For that reason, we are glad to have a good, gay-sensitive, and knowledgeable attorney, sound wills, reliable executors, powers of attorney, health care proxies, and a prenuptial agreement. We have yet to arrange for our funerals, but given John's experience, we will do so soon.

According to information provided by GLAD, the Boston-based lesbian and gay nonprofit legal organization, every gay and lesbian couple should have the following basic protections:

• Estate Planning. This includes wills and trusts. In the absence of a will, all assets are transferred to one's next of kin. Trusts provide significant tax benefits for couples with complicated estates.

• Relationship Agreement. Also called "prenuptial," "antenuptial," or "cohabitation" agreement, it ensures that both parties agree on their rights and duties, and outlines what will happen if the couple splits up.

• Durable Power of Attorney. This gives one partner the right to make financial decisions for the other, should he or she be unable to do so. Without this document, next of kin has this right.

• Health Care Proxy. Also called "health care power of attorney," this delegates the right to make health care decisions on behalf of a partner who is incapable of doing so. It also ensures access to the hospitalized partner and to her or his physicians.

As needed, gay and lesbian couples should also have:

• Guardianship Papers. These ensure that a child will remain with the surviving partner in the event of the other's death.

• Parenting Agreement. This outlines each partner's obligations and decision-making rights with regard to a child. It also details visitation rights and support obligations, should the couple break up.

• Co-parent Adoption. Also called "second parent adoption," this protects the parental rights of nonbiological parents in relationships with biological parents.

• Alternative Insemination Agreement. This outlines the rights and responsibilities of the sperm donor or surrogate (egg donor) regarding the child or children to be conceived through alternative insemination.

• Real Estate Agreement. This provides for how property will be held and how mortgage and maintenance will be paid. It states what will happen to the property should the relationship end. (This can be part of the Relationship Agreement.)

GLAD reminds us that the laws vary from state to state; thus not every document may hold up in court. It is essential that gay and lesbian couples get legal advice.

Most of the necessary documents can be secured inexpensively, but to save time and money couples should think through their needs prior to contacting an attorney. Organizations like GLAD and Lambda, which handle test cases but don't have the resources to provide direct legal services, are happy to make referrals to private attorneys, some of whom may work for reduced fees or pro bono.

Beyond all of the legal fuss, for which I have great use but no mind, is the bottom-line issue of glorious gay and lesbian love. That is the treasure of which we must never lose sight.

Ray and I might not live long enough to be able to visit all fifty states and have our relationship treated with legal respect. We may spend many years being bombarded with mean-spirited, demeaning comments by uninformed people about their perceptions of our love. We may even suffer physically because of the frightening backlash created by the nastiness of those who oppose us on the marriage issue. But none of it can take away from us the beautiful love we share, nor destroy the unique, living entity we have created. Only we can do that.

Black people were in holy union with black people all the while they were forbidden to be married by white society. The Supreme Court did not give legitimacy to the love whites had for their Asian mates. Closing the church doors on Catholics who committed themselves in love to Jews didn't make their love void.

The church and the state do not have the power to define what is love or what is a union of two souls. They can only give support or deny support. The support is nice—it can make life a lot easier—but it is not essential. That has always been and will always be true.

We know it has always been true because we have seen proof of it. Gay and lesbian lovers throughout history have left us indelible testimonies of their unsanctioned relationships, and Ray and I take great pleasure in finding and collecting some of those bold, brave statements.

The New York Metropolitan Museum of Art contains several, but my very favorite is a Roman goblet to which I make a regular pilgrimage. Beautifully depicted on both sides of this first-century cup are male lovers in unabashed coital embrace. (An accompanying note explains that the anonymously donated piece had been withheld from public view until recently because of the subject matter.)

As I gratefully explore every detail of the silver drinking vessel, I am awed by my intense sense of connection with the man who had the cup made, who held it in his hand and brought it to his lips. He and his artisan left for me an ancient image of my love and sensuality that has survived centuries of persecution. We are one in spirit.

Ray and I felt a similar awe and communion as we embraced the adjacent tombstones of lesbian lovers Gertrude Stein and Alice B. Toklas on a wooded hill of the Cimetière du Père-Lachaise overlooking Paris.

About Alice, Gertrude once wrote:

> I caught sight of a splendid Misses. She had handkerchiefs and kisses. She had eyes and yellow shoes, she had everything to choose, and she chose me. In passing through France she wore a Chinese hat and so did I. In looking at the sun she read a map. And so did I. In eating fish and pork she grew fat. And so did I. In loving a blue sea she had a pain. And so did I. How prettily we swim. Not in water. Not on land. But in love."[9]

I recall that when we noted on their graves how Gertrude had preceded Alice in death by many years, we felt both intense sadness over their long separation, but pure joy over their ultimate, planned reunion.

Their inspiring love is celebrated for us not only by the treasured memories of our quiet time with them in the cemetery but also by the frequent sight of their books "kissing" on the shelf in my office. Gertrude's *Three Lives*[10] and Alice's *What Is Remembered*[11] will be joined together for as long as we live.

So too will be the names of Victor Amburgy and Jack McCarty, the brave male lovers who were among the TWA passengers held hostage for seventeen days by Shiite hijackers. Their inspiring story of tender devotion through the horrors of that ordeal continues to influence our lives. Though Victor and Jack were later separated from one another by AIDS, their romantic union is immortalized for us and for future generations by their signatures on our gay and lesbian poster of pride.

A gift from Lily Tomlin many years ago, the autographed poster of the film *The Late Show* has been transformed into a wall-mounted "guest book" for gay and lesbian friends who are active in the movement. Among the lovers who have joined Victor and Jack in this testimony are Dave McWhirter and Drew Mattison, Lynn Lavner and Ardis Sperber, and Tom Wilson Weinberg and John Whyte.

Across from this wonderful poster is the captivating sepia photograph of what appear to be five handsome gay male couples taken about one hundred and fifty years ago. Supposedly found in an attic in New England, and now displayed in what we assume is its original frame, the picture inspires everyone who visits our home.

"Oh my God, look at their faces," people will say. "They're so much in love!"

Each man, dressed stylishly but not formally in waistcoat and tie, sits or stands next to what seems to be his beloved. Some are gently connected by the touch of their hands; others rest their head lovingly on the broad shoulder of their mate.

In our search, we have found other incredible signs of unapproved gay love in paintings, pottery, poetry, tree trunk carvings, and graffiti, among other places. Like the words of Ruth to Naomi, and Gertrude to Alice, they were all left by people who dared to love another of the same sex, didn't have permission to do so, and refused to keep it a secret.

I truly believe that one day this gay and lesbian love will be afforded the same legal protections and benefits given to heterosexuals. Change in the laws regarding gay marriage will eventually come as a result of our hard work. Until then, we all need to protect ourselves from the discrimination imposed by the state the best we can with what is available to us.

But the most important thing we can do for ourselves is celebrate today and always the natural beauty and goodness of our gay and lesbian love. And maybe leave for those who follow a sign that we, our lovers, and our love were here.

One day, a long time from now, I suspect a gay or lesbian couple, killing time on a rainy Saturday afternoon, will come across my New American Bible in a secondhand bookstore. I see them laughing with delight at my quaint entry under "Certificate of Marriage." And then, with a sympathetic look of wonder, one will ask the other, "What do you think it was like to be a gay couple back then?"

"One can only imagine," the other will respond thoughtfully. "But it's sure clear to me that these two loved one another."

5

ABOUT
THE WORKPLACE

James Dobson and Donald Wildmon, among other fundamentalist commentators, are quite upset by the kind of transformation that occurred in a midwestern AT&T facility in the middle of the night, and they don't hesitate to say so.

I, on the other hand, am very pleased and excited.

It happened in a workshop. The participant list was made up of the factory's third shift, and most of the people were not thrilled about being there, myself included. My training partner, Pam Wilson, and I weren't used to starting an eight-hour session at 10:30 P.M., nor to being greeted by so many unsmiling faces.

We were told in advance by the group's supervisor that there had been a major, unprecedented confrontation with some of the employees over their attendance at the program "Gay Issues in the Workplace." They didn't want to go. It was "an assault on their values," some reportedly said. But begrudgingly the disgruntled union members ultimately agreed to sit through at least the first hour of the diversity training.

Among the participants, we were advised, was a man thought to be gay whose poor attendance at work was cause for considerable management concern. Speculation was that he felt unsafe because his job environment was so homophobic. Pam's and my task was to help change that environment.

None of the standard light-hearted lines in my introduction worked very well to break the ice with this group. Instead of the usual broad smiles and friendly laughter, I mostly saw pursed lips and was confronted by unsettling silence. A quick look to Pam's rolling eyes assured me that it wasn't my imagination.

Reminding myself of the program's successful track record, however, I stayed the course, and as the evening proceeded the participants indeed began to relax, to smile, to look engaged, and even to laugh. One by one they started uncrossing their arms and legs and communicating with a nod that they understood my points.

Except for the man in the second row on the left. His face was beet red. His arms and legs remained tightly crossed. His squinted eyes glared defiantly at the wall in front of the room, and he refused any sign of engagement in the workshop. His sole focus seemed to be the quickly expiring hour.

Most of the group heard me explain the company's interest in creating a safe and productive work environment for everyone. They listened to definitions and examples of heterosexism and homophobia, as well as to an explanation of the negative impact these have on productivity. I underscored that we sought to change people's inappropriate *behaviors* at work, not their *moral values*. I added that the discomfort one feels with homosexuality is generally due to lack of exposure.

"Often people make and laugh at negative comments about

gay people," I explained, "not knowing how unfair, uninformed, and hurtful the jokes and laughter are."

To counteract that, I told them, Pam and I would be providing them accurate information about homosexuality, creating empathy for the victims of anti-gay bias, and enhancing their skills to appropriately respond to such hostile behaviors.

Finally, I assured them that everything we said was "being offered for their consideration," that there was no such thing as a dumb question, and that we wanted them to freely express their thoughts and feelings throughout the evening.

The first hour was up and everyone stayed seated.

It was Pam's turn now. She had the participants assemble in front of the room and stand before the flip chart at the position that best captured their response to her questions.

"How would you describe the atmosphere in your work environment for gay, lesbian, and bisexual employees?" she asked. "Is it 'very hostile,' 'somewhat hostile,' 'somewhat accepting,' or 'very accepting?' "

The majority of the group stood at the "hostile" end of the continuum. They reported hearing lots of mean-spirited jokes and comments from coworkers about homosexuals.

"If a coworker that you really liked told you that she or he was gay," Pam continued, "what do you think would be best for that person, given your perception of the environment? Should the person 'stay in the closet,' 'come out to a few close friends,' 'come out to their supervisor,' or 'come out to everyone?' "

"I'd sure stay in the closet around here," said the angry man from the second row on the left, now standing at the "hostile" end of the spectrum. "I couldn't promise that someone's hands wouldn't get cut off in the machines if someone said that they were gay."

"Really?" Pam responded, as our eyes met in disbelief.

Neither of us knew who of the other employees was thought to be gay, so we couldn't look to that person for a physical sign of reaction. Two or three employees immediately jumped on the statement, though, challenging the perception of such extreme hostility.

"What are you *talking* about?" asked one.

The group as a whole then began a lively dialogue, with many of them insisting that their workplace was far more tolerant than was being characterized. One or two spoke up about having a gay friend or relative whom they liked or loved.

As we anticipated, and so heavily counted upon, the workshop attendees no longer saw themselves as a monolithic group having nothing in common with the topic. Their courage to speak up and break ranks was given a boost when they were confronted with an image of their darkest side. Most of them wanted no part of it. They wanted to think of themselves as fair-minded Americans, not bigots.

Particularly appealing to them was hearing that they could be supportive of gay issues at work and still maintain their religious convictions. "Anybody could be an ally," they heard.

The training proceeded with generally predictable, though always gratifying, success as the participants clarified their understanding of human sexuality, learned that sexual orientation is not a choice, and came to realize from my personal story how frightening it can be to grow up gay or lesbian with a "secret you don't understand, and are afraid to share with anyone for fear that they won't love or respect you anymore."

"That holds true for many of the gay and lesbian people who work among you," they were told. "They grew up in homes in which they were afraid, they went to schools in which they were afraid, and now they report daily to this factory in which they are afraid to share with you their true identity."

By 6:30 the following morning, we felt secure that we had helped the factory workers in attendance understand why the issue was important to the company and how they could be helpful in creating a more tolerant and tolerable environment for their gay, lesbian, and bisexual colleagues. They now had enough knowledge and sufficient skills to identify and respond to the problem. The rest was up to them and to their management.

A day later, the group's supervisor, who had sat through the workshop with them, called excitedly to tell me his good news.

"I thought you'd like to know," he said, "that after you and Pam left the room, Bill, that guy in the second row who was so uncomfortable, goes up to Tom, the guy everyone thinks is gay, and says, 'Are you gay?'

"Tom was real nervous but he answers, 'Yeah, I am.'

"Then Bill says, 'Well, I'm sorry for all of the stuff I've said.' "

What transpired between those two workers is the hope of the gay civil rights movement. *How* it happened is our best route to the future. And both are precisely what make conservative religious talk show hosts and other spokespersons so uncomfortable. While they may not know the details and aftermath of this particular training, they are well aware of what is going on in corporate America today and they don't like it one bit.

Gay, lesbian, and bisexual employees across the country are asking for their employers' help in creating a safer, more productive, more equitable workplace in which they will be treated with professional respect, and be evaluated on the basis of their skills and performance, not on their sexual orientation.

Gay employees don't want to come to work and worry all day (or night) that coming out of the closet will mean, among other things, that someone loses his or her hands in a machine, is described as a "fag" or "dyke" on the john wall or in cafeteria discussions, finds a deep key-scratch or broken window in their car, or is greeted by a condemning biblical quote in their work station.

My guess is that though these Christian fundamentalist leaders don't consciously want their heterosexual followers to harass gay coworkers in such ways, it makes them very nervous that a heterosexual, such as Bill, might become openly friendly to, and supportive of, a gay person, such as Tom. They don't trust the ability of their audience to distinguish between *acceptance* of gay people and *endorsement* of homosexuality.

Likewise, those who oppose basic civil rights for gay Americans are threatened by efforts to instill *self-esteem* in gay, lesbian, and bisexual people. Preferring that gay people like Tom see and conduct themselves as helpless *victims* in need of "salvation," they abhor the concept of gay pride and dismiss those who speak up for themselves as "militants" or "activists" with an "agenda."

That is why they so strongly oppose corporate-sponsored education on gay issues in the workplace. And with good reason. They know that a thoughtful presentation on the impact of homophobia on productivity effectively makes professional allies out of most heterosexual coworkers and engenders in most gay employees a healthy sense of self.

"As a result of your seminar," wrote a heterosexual woman after one such training, "one member of our division decided to 'come out' to close friends and his manager. This is a difficult and moving process for all of us, but I know I am better prepared than I was [before]."

"Even though I have never experienced much of what he described," stated another employee in a postworkshop evaluation of my presentation, "he touched on common feelings I think all people have. This evoked a very strong response from me and helped me to see gay people in a more realistic way."

Still another said, "This is an issue I was quite uncomfortable about, and I was apprehensive about today's meeting. But this was one of the most . . . helpful sessions in years for me. It was thought-provoking both for our work environment and in terms of my family and kids."

In response to these educational programs, conservative radio talk show host Dobson has been repeatedly urging his *Focus on the Family* listeners to strongly pressure corporations such as AT&T, Disney, and Coors, among others, to stop "endorsing the gay lifestyle." Thousands of people have subsequently called and written these companies threatening a boycott.

Wildmon, president of the American Family Association, has urged his members to switch to a "Christian" long-distance carrier because AT&T, among other reasons, "indoctrinates their employees to accept homosexuality using the video *On Being Gay* by homosexual activist Brian McNaught."

As most observers on both sides of the gay civil rights issue agree, corporate America is now the battleground on which gay, lesbian, and bisexual people currently have the best opportunity to make the most significant, long-term gains. This is true, I believe, even considering the monumental issue of gay marriage.

From Maine to Hawaii, gay people are coming out at work in unprecedented numbers. We are forming groups inside and outside the workplace and asking for fair treatment on the job. Gay employee resource groups, business associations, and professional affiliations are now the largest, fastest-growing, and most energetic, focused, and some would argue *vital* organizations in the community.

Motivated by profit and unencumbered by religious tradition or legal restrictions, many corporations are responding to the requests of these gay organizations with a reasonableness not generally found in the community's dialogue with the church or state. These employers understand that *all* workers need a safe and just corporate environment in order to work cooperatively and enthusiastically with others. Businesses today realize that the effectiveness of their work teams correlates directly to their competitiveness in the marketplace. So it makes good business sense to create an environment where gay, lesbian, and bisexual employees can be fully functioning members of work teams without having to hide their true identities.

The needs of gay employees have been clearly stated in the abundance of books now available on gay issues in the workplace, as well as by the Wall Street Project,[1] and V Management's "Lavender Screen Test."[2] They are:

1. A widely distributed and seriously addressed policy that prohibits discrimination based upon sexual orientation in recruiting, hiring, training, and promoting into all job levels;

2. A comprehensive, fully supported educational program for employees at all levels on gay issues in the workplace, to complement diversity training on race, gender, and religion, among others;

3. A gay, lesbian, and bisexual business resource group (BRG) that, like other BRGs, serves to support its members, represent their concerns to management, educate the workforce, and represent the company's product to outside constituents;

4. Spousal benefits to the domestic partners of gay, lesbian, and bisexual employees, equal to those provided to spouses of heterosexual employees;

5. A strongly enforced, well-distributed policy that prohibits discrimination against employees with HIV and AIDS.

Gay employees also want their companies to indicate interest in and support of the community through advertising and sponsorship of gay-related events, such as the Gay Games and the AIDS Walk, as they do to other minority groups. In addition, we want our employers to "walk the talk" of nondiscrimination by standing firm against the opposition to their policies and practices from inside and outside the company.

These are now the very issues over which religious fundamentalists are rallying their troops. Disney, for instance, is being boycotted for providing domestic partner benefits to gay employees. Dobson is heavily pressuring AT&T to excuse people from diversity training on gay issues, and Wildmon is angry about AT&T's advertising outreach to gay customers and its support of the Gay Games.

It is clearly the hope of the radical right that corporations, like elected representatives, can be forced into compliance. They sense they can win their battle in the arena of public opinion, believing that fear of economic loss will persuade companies to back off on gay issues. And if the officers of the corporation can't be intimidated, they mount efforts to influence stockholders.

Nevertheless, the progress made by gay people in the workplace in the last decade is dizzying. The list of companies that prohibit discrimination based on sexual orientation grows longer every day. The Internet is constantly filled with news of yet another corporation providing domestic partner benefits to its gay, lesbian, and bisexual workers. And gay business resource groups are either in formation or are well established in a hundred major corporations.

Many gay people sense that the train has left the station and there is no stopping the rapid advances being made in the workplace. There is a giddiness that finally a battle is being won.

I share the enthusiasm but fear that in our excitement over short-term successes, we risk losing focus on our greatest opportunity for global and lasting change: namely, the chance to create true understanding of and support for our issues among both gay and straight workers, like Tom and Bill.

Of the five basic needs on our list to employers, the most significant, and often the lowest in priority, is education. While the other issues of concern are all very important, the most critical ingredient for creating a truly safe and productive work environment is diversity training.

If we don't understand, prioritize, and mount resources to generate and support corporate-wide education, we direct our fast-moving train down a dead-end track. We end up with policies that aren't enforced, benefits that aren't utilized, gay employees who stay closeted, and heterosexual coworkers who still feel threatened and angry. Regrettably, some gay and lesbian employees, local business associations, and national organizations at times lost sight of this.

Clearly, corporate nondiscrimination policies that include sexual orientation are essential to creating an equal playing field for gay, lesbian, and bisexual employees. Getting such policies written, adopted, and disseminated needs to be a top priority for all justice- and productivity-oriented businesses. Yet, we should never delude ourselves into thinking that having the policy in place will actually end bias in the workplace.

I know of companies with such policies in which openly lesbian and gay employees are subjected to all manner of discrimination, including physical harassment. In order for a policy to positively impact the everyday life of the gay employee it has to be enforced. To be enforced, it has to be understood and supported. Nondiscrimination policies have no legal standing outside of the company. They are statements of management's intent. Nothing more.

A nondiscrimination policy regarding HIV and AIDS is also very important. Although most gay men, lesbian women, and bisexual people are not HIV-positive, their communities have been disproportionately affected by the epidemic. For this reason, most gay employees feel safest when their company has a nondiscrimination policy regarding HIV and AIDS.

The value here, as before, however, is in having a statement of intent that is widely disseminated, understood, and enforced. Legally, HIV-positive people and those with AIDS are protected against discrimination by the Americans with Disabilities Act (ADA). A company policy on AIDS is basically an educational tool. In and of itself it is not enough.

I have worked with companies that have such policies and that also have employees who refuse to work on the same terminal as a gay man or lesbian woman for fear of contracting AIDS. The company's policy and federal law have done little to alleviate those fears. What is clearly needed is education.

Having a gay business resource group is another important ingredient for the gay person seeking safety and support at work. These are an invaluable means of networking professionally as well as socially, and can help the employee address concerns to management.

Gay and lesbian BRGs are the prime motivating force for securing policies and benefits. They also can be and need to be a catalyst for, and source of, education on gay issues in the workplace. Many gay BRGs, for instance, lobby their human resources (HR) professionals to provide ongoing diversity education, as well as sponsor their own programs such as Gay Awareness Month noon-hour talks and video presentations.

Finally, BRG members can be effective public relations and marketing representatives for their corporation in the gay, lesbian, and bisexual communities.

As important as these groups are, however, they should not be thought of by either management or the group itself as being *responsible* for the corporation's commitment to addressing gay and lesbian workplace issues. The BRG members all have their own demanding jobs that make it impossible for them to dedicate themselves full-time to that task. On the other hand, human resources professionals, as well as all managers, are mandated by their job descriptions to ensure a safe and equitable work environment for all employees.

Domestic partner benefits are another issue of major concern to openly gay job seekers. Beyond being allowed to acknowledge their sexual orientation in the workplace, gay, lesbian, and bisexual employees want to receive the same compensation and consideration as their heterosexual counterparts. If they are coupled, the inadequacy of their benefits package, when compared to that of married heterosexual coworkers, is particularly blatant and troublesome.

Currently, these domestic partner benefits have taken on enormous significance among gay employees. They have become the prime topic of discussion in meetings between the leadership of many gay BRGs and management. Denial of benefits is experienced as proof that the company favors its heterosexual workers and is not serious about eliminating bias based upon sexual orientation. Granting of benefits is experienced as the company "walking the talk" of its commitment to its gay employees.

There is no disputing the major political significance of a corporation's providing domestic partner benefits to its gay, lesbian, and bisexual employees. It sends a message not only to gay employees and to their heterosexual colleagues, but to consumers as well, that the company is committed to the fair treatment of its homosexual workers.

In domestic partner benefits, gay people also finally receive from their employer what they are unable to get from most churches and, until recently, from any state: a recognition of the legitimacy of their loving commitment to another. The psychological impact and social implications of receiving those benefits are enormous.

That said, if gay, lesbian, and bisexual employees had to choose between getting domestic partner benefits from their company or getting a commitment to long-term education of employees on gay issues, the choice should be for education.

In those companies that provide domestic partner benefits, less than one percent of the estimated gay workforce has signed up for them. While receiving health care benefits for a loved one is a lifesaving issue for some gay, lesbian, and bisexual employees, the vast majority don't appear to be interested in them beyond their symbolic value. Their lovers are already covered by policies at their place of employment; they don't want to pay taxes on the additional income the benefits represent; they don't want to have to come out of the closet to sign up for them; or they're single.

Despite that, many members of gay BRGs prioritize securing the benefits over keeping the feet of human resources professionals to the fire about diversity education. When given the opportunity to quiz a member of management, the questions too often are about "When are we going to get benefits?" rather than "Have you educated yourself and your staff about gay issues? If 'yes,' how so?" If that member of management had a good diversity education about gay workplace issues, he or she might not need to be repeatedly prodded about benefits.

Education is essential to creating a safe, equitable, and productive work environment in which gay employees will feel able and eager to come out and in which heterosexual employees will enthusiastically support corporate efforts to eliminate bias.

I know that. The leadership of the radical right knows that. And I believe that most gay, lesbian, and bisexual people do too.

I suspect that the reason why few gay, lesbian, and bisexual people want to acknowledge this is that education about homosexuality is a long, slow, difficult process nowhere near as initially exciting or as instantly gratifying as a nondiscrimination policy or domestic partner benefits.

Yet, we know that if we want to work side by side with heterosexuals who don't make offensive comments about homosexuality and don't feel enormous resentment about the company's nondiscrimination policy, domestic partner benefits, gay business resource group, HIV employment policy, and the nasty public debate that accompanies all of them, we need to prioritize education.

Proof of this for me comes from my experience as a trainer. In those corporate facilities in which we are just initiating workshops on gay issues, there is generally a high level of resistance, like that we found among the factory's third shift employees. As with them, the majority of participants stand at the "hostile" end of the continuum to describe their work environment. However, in those facilities in which we have conducted extensive training, the majority of the participants stand at the "accepting" end of the continuum.

"It used to be really bad around here," they will say. "But since they started this workshop, things have changed."

Things have changed, as we know, because many heterosexuals were given their first opportunity to understand who their gay, lesbian, and bisexual colleagues are and what they want and need to feel safe and valued in the workplace. Those who have been educated about homosexuality can become effective allies in the battle for mutual respect at work.

"I realize that I will never fully comprehend just how difficult, frustrating, and scary it must be for young homosexual people to grow up in a mostly heterosexual world, but . . . I now have been sensitized to the issues they face in their day-to-day lives," wrote one male employee after a training. "I only hope that I can be one of the people who are willing to stand up and say 'enough, already' when someone starts spouting an offensive joke, or puts somebody down because they're different than the majority."

The new sensitivity that results from effective training can also include a better understanding of the issue of domestic partner benefits. Until they are made aware of the full implications of what it means to be gay, heterosexuals have a hard time being supportive of the company providing health care to the "sex partners" of their gay coworkers.

"It cheapens marriage and will bring upon the downfall of western civilization," insisted one angry employee.

But when they are enabled to see the significance of the loving, committed relationship to the gay employee, heterosexual coworkers then generally support their gay colleagues' getting bereavement leave, and health care benefits for their partners. When allowed to hear the reasoning behind the issue, heterosexual workers can better identify with gay people's claim that we are not getting "equal pay for equal work."

They don't get that understanding from a desk-to-desk memo from the manager, advising them of a new company policy. It only comes when they are given the chance to articulate their fears, to learn accurate information, and to resolve their concerns.

Then why doesn't corporate diversity education always get the time, attention, and resources it needs and deserves from gay and lesbian employees, business associations, and national organizations? Partly, I suspect, because it lacks immediate and sustained gratification, but mostly because it is often difficult to sell to timid executives and nervous human resources professionals, and their interest is especially hard to maintain.

When the idea of corporate-wide diversity training is first taken up as a goal by a gay and lesbian business resource group there is almost always a wonderful flurry of activity. Research is done. Meetings are held with human resources personnel and department managers to build the case for education. Pilot programs are arranged. And with a sigh of relief, everyone celebrates the overwhelmingly positive feedback on the post-workshop evaluations. Success.

But then boredom and burnout can set in. The gay BRG may want a new challenge or may step back out of exhaustion. And the human resources or diversity professionals, unless personally connected with, or otherwise committed to, the issue, can feel threatened and worn down by the vocal opposition being generated against the classes. They can also feel unsupported by an ambivalent and uneasy management, and now under no pressure from the gay employees to maintain the training.

"The whole thing just collapsed," explained Jill Olkoski, the dynamic leader of one of her company's local business resource groups. "In the beginning it was great. People were enthused. The training was a big success. But then, the handful of us that had been pushing the HR people to offer the workshop got burned out. We couldn't get any other gay employees to pick up the slack. So, now there's nothing.

"Straight coworkers have been coming up to me to say how sorry they are that there's no longer any training," she continued. "They said it made a big difference around here. It did. People started coming out. People started talking about their family members and friends who were gay. Not anymore.

"One guy, in particular, who had really been moved by the training, asked if there was anything he could do. I told him to call the HR office," she said. "But ultimately it's my community's responsibility. I'm okay saying that it's our job. We have to fight for what's near and dear to our hearts. But I got burned out, and I couldn't get anyone else involved."

While I want to disagree with Jill about its being her responsibility to ensure that her colleagues get training on gay issues in the workplace, I do feel that the training often won't be initiated or maintained without the involvement of gay and lesbian employees.

No one can deny that openly gay, lesbian, and bisexual people entering the job market, or changing their professional direction, have more opportunities today to find a safe and productive environment than ever before. While our homosexual ancestors who rejected life in the closet often felt limited to certain careers—in the arts and design, for example—surveys today show there are more openly gay people employed as engineers than as interior decorators, librarians, hairdressers, or florists.

Now, gay people can find not only a state or city that guarantees them protection against discrimination, but also employers in most every conceivable field that promise they will do the same. Though one may need to do some research to find the best opportunities, there is nothing to stop an openly gay person from following his or her dreams into almost any profession.

You may not be able to be an openly gay teacher in the school in which you were educated, but if you're qualified there's a place in the country where you can teach. You can also be an openly gay or lesbian rabbi or nun, doctor, firefighter, coach, or investment banker. You may have to move to another state, another work site, or even another church at this time, but the options are numerous and are becoming more plentiful daily.

What takes place once the openly gay, lesbian, or bisexual person secures that job, however, is another matter entirely. In order for these workers to truly feel safe and valued, and to be treated equally, their colleagues need a comprehensive diversity training on gay issues in the workplace.

For that to happen, all gay employees need to be prepared to lobby for the initiation and maintenance of this educational process. This is true everywhere in the country.

"Not where I live and work," I have heard some gay people argue. "Everyone here is cool on the gay issue. It's not a problem."

I would be glad for that, but I don't trust the perception.

A few years ago, I was invited to San Francisco to speak to a corporate audience on homosexuality. I thought to myself, "They've got to be kidding. *San Francisco!* What can I tell them that they don't already know?"

It was, as I recall, a bright sunny day at the time of the workshop. We assembled in a civic center auditorium with state-of-the-art audiovisual aids and very comfortable seats. The professionally dressed group of upper managers chatted together lightheartedly.

Just prior to my taking the stage, a shabbily dressed, unshaven homeless person moved quickly to the front of the room and began speaking loudly to the startled group.

"Excuse me everyone," he said, his eyes darting around the room. "May I please have your attention. I am not a threat to you. If everyone will relax, everything will be alright. I have in my pocket . . ."

He was now surrounded by several anxious-looking security guards, who firmly but politely asked him to leave. The faces of members of the audience registered alarm.

"Please let go of me," he said, shaking off the arm of one guard. "I am homeless but I mean you no harm. I have in my pocket a prescription for medication. I need twenty dollars to pay for that medication. I am not crazy. I am Harvard educated. I . . ."

As the guards now more forcefully were pulling him off the stage, I went forward and gave the man twenty dollars. He thanked me and left quietly.

The room was buzzing. I began to speak.

"It was scary, wasn't it?" I asked, my own heart pounding. "None of us knew what to do. Was he dangerous? Was he lying?

95

Did we just get ripped off? Will he spend the money on medicine?"

People nodded in recognition of their shared concerns.

"Ignorance is the parent of fear. We all felt anxious because we don't have any exposure to the issue. We didn't trust our instincts. We didn't want to do the wrong thing. We didn't want to look like fools. Yet, we wanted to feel good about how we handled the situation. We wished someone would tell us how to respond to these situations. Is that right?"

"Yes," many responded with smiles of relief.

"That's the way some of us feel about the gay issue too," I continued. "We feel anxious because we don't know what we're doing. We're afraid to ask what seem like silly questions because we don't want to be offensive or to look like fools—especially in San Francisco! We also don't want to compromise our values. Yet, we want to do the right thing. We wish someone would tell us how to handle uncomfortable situations. Does that sound familiar?"

Big smiles now. "He understands."

What I came to understand as a result of that training was that many of the heterosexual members of this sophisticated audience in San Francisco were as ill-informed about the issue of homosexuality as most of those on the third shift in the midwestern factory. They were just less anxious and a bit less forthcoming about it.

The Bay Area managers knew they were expected to be supportive on gay issues but they didn't have the benefit of any better sex education than did their union counterparts. While they undoubtedly had more gay, lesbian, bisexual, and transgender friends than their colleagues in places like Conyers, Georgia, they didn't understand an awful lot more about what makes someone gay, or about how orientation, for instance, differs from gender identity. They still wanted to know, "Is it a choice?" and "Do lesbians think of themselves as men?" As a result, though the social norms of San Francisco and the corporate guidelines of their employer dictated that they be professional and cordial with gay colleagues, many of these heterosexual men and women had a difficult time feeling completely comfortable with them.

Remarkably, the gay people in the audience were not all that different from their counterparts throughout the country, either. While they may have trusted that they could come out without "someone's hands getting cut off in the machines," some of them were still reluctant to do so. They correctly didn't trust that their colleagues really understood why they would feel the need to identify themselves as gay, lesbian, or bisexual.

It was a good lesson for me to learn about human nature and the universal importance and impact of education. No matter where it happens, and under what circumstances, on a bright sunny day in San Francisco or in the middle of the night in a midwestern factory, people grow when they are allowed and encouraged to do so.

The truth of that statement is what ultimately will prevent religious political extremists from stopping the gay civil rights movement. When people are empowered through education, they are able to make decisions and distinctions for themselves. Boycotts and other threats by fundamentalist pedagogues can't stop that liberating process. They can only stop the training itself.

Just prior to a recent trip back to the midwestern factory, I had a conversation with the human resources manager that helped underscore these beliefs.

"How are Bill and Tom doing?" I asked.

"Funny you should ask," she said. "You'll love this. Tom, he was the guy who wouldn't come to work, well, he called and asked to meet with me. Seems things were getting bad again with Bill."

"That's too bad," I said.

"Well, wait. There's more," she continued. "He didn't show up for our meeting, so I called him. He says, 'Oh, it's okay. I took care of it myself.' "

"What did he mean?" I asked.

"He said that he confronted Bill with how his comments were affecting him. And he reports that Bill said "Sorry, I'll stop."

"Wow! Good for them," I said.

"Yeah," she replied. "Good for all of us."

6

ABOUT
OUR FAMILIES

On the occasion of his twenty-first birthday, I wrote a column about my younger brother. I called it "Am Twice-Blessed by Brother, Friend."

"Mom prefers that I refer to my younger brother as 'Tom,' " I wrote, "because adulthood entitles him to put away the things of a child. But he has always been Tommy to me and I suppose always will be.

"As I once wrote Tommy, some men are blessed with best friends, others are blessed with brothers. I have been twice-blessed."

Since childhood, my brother and I have been closer than any two members of the family. Separated in age by only two years, we shared a bedroom, clothes, and friends for most of our adolescence. In my bedroom today proudly hangs a photograph of us holding hands. I was five and he was three and we were dressed alike. Tommy displays a similar photograph in his home.

Far from inseparable, we were sometimes at each other's throats, particularly as we entered our teenage years. Both very competitive, we were raised in a family where you generally heard of the accomplishments of others, as opposed to your own. Tom and I competed for the praise of our parents, grandparents, our Aunt Joan, and our teachers. We were both altar boys, patrol boys, scouts, and good students. We were also both organizers of our high school class homecoming floats and our class field day activities. We both were senior class presidents and yearbook editors, he in high school, I in college.

For most of high school, Tommy dated Mary Bird and I dated Jody Cronyn. They never met, as we never double-dated. By that age we had separate friends. Although we both went to Marquette University, as our father had before us, we kept a friendly distance until my senior year, when Tom joined me on the yearbook staff.

To my father's chagrin, Tommy and I were both liberal Democrats and, like many of our generation, we passionately opposed the war in Vietnam. I recall vividly how Tommy sat with me, as did the other yearbook staff members, when the first draft lottery numbers were announced over the radio. We were all quite shaken when my number was called, my brother particularly so.

Later, when the draft board recognized my conscientious objector status, Tom proudly gave me a pewter mug engraved with the poignant words of Robert Frost: "Two roads diverged in a wood, and I— / I took the one less traveled by, / And that has made all the difference."

I was a member of Eugene McCarthy's children's crusade. Tom gave his fervent support to Bobby Kennedy in his run for the Democratic presidential nomination. I remember how devastated and confused Tommy was as he sat in silence for three days in the basement of our home watching the television coverage of his hero's assassination and funeral. I ached for him.

Yet, despite our mutual love and support, despite having shared seemingly every intimate detail of our lives for most of our youth, there was one thing I couldn't tell Tommy. That was my secret about being physically attracted to men.

I worried that if my younger brother knew I was homosexual it would frighten him or make him ashamed of me. I feared losing his love and respect. So when I wrote my loving tribute to him in *The Michigan Catholic,* I did so in my closet.

A few years later, after I had lost my job at the paper for being gay and was living with my new partner, Ray, in Boston, Tommy arrived for what he insisted would be a short visit. "I'm on my way to Ireland to backpack," he said. "I'll only be here for the weekend."

Six months later he got his own apartment.

Within the first week, Tom announced: "Brian, I'm gay too. You tell Mom and Dad. You're better with words than I am."

I'd had only the faintest suspicion about Tommy. He always had a girlfriend and talked of having had heterosexual sex. In college he took an overdose of pills, but I accepted his explanation of depression from the pressures of school.

During my civil rights case with *The Michigan Catholic,* Tom was conspicuously silent. I felt abandoned, not understanding why he kept his distance. It turns out he was in a loving, sexual relationship with another male graduate student and feared that the camera lights on me might catch his shadow.

Mom and Dad were confused, disappointed, and skeptical when they learned that Tom was gay. They had come to accept my homosexuality—if not my vocation as gay writer and speaker—and they truly liked Ray. But Tommy being gay was quite another issue.

Was it my influence? they wondered. Was it a phase? Could he know for sure? Once again they were forced to question their parenting skills, to worry about a child's happiness, and to grieve the loss of their dreams. They also questioned the wisdom of Tom living with Ray and me.

Whether or not Mom and Dad realized it, though—and I suspect they eventually did—Tom was in the best possible place he could be. Ray's and my home has always been a wonderful, safe gathering space for gay, lesbian, bisexual, and transgender people from all walks of life. While living with us, Tommy met and talked with politicians, writers, house painters, newscasters, priests, hustlers, nuns, coaches, and movie stars. He met "in your face" homosexuals and those in the closet, transsexuals and transvestites, people in long-term monogamous relationships and celebrated singles. He also met an abundance of heterosexual allies.

The experience of living with us challenged his preconceived ideas of what it meant to be gay and provided him with role models for integrating his sexual orientation into his life. It was a healthy, nurturing environment I wish I'd had when I was coming out. I wish it for everyone who is gay, lesbian, or bisexual.

According to a study by Dr. Richard Pillard at Boston University's School of Medicine, approximately twenty percent of gay men and ten percent of lesbians have a gay sibling.[1] So it is possible that a significant number of gay people have been, or could be, "birthed" into their gay life by the loving hands of a gay brother or sister. I have met many gay men and women who have gay siblings. Some of my friends have two or three gay people in their immediate family. I even know of a family of five brothers, all of whom are gay.

Understandably, not all gay people with gay siblings are close to them. In some cases, they don't like them. The same obviously holds true for heterosexual siblings. But most of the gay people I know with a gay brother or lesbian sister are thrilled to have gay kin. Without much prodding, they tell wonderfully funny and moving stories about how they came out to each other.

They also often say that their lives would be less fulfilling without their gay sibling.

I love having a brother who is gay. Growing up feeling isolated from the rest of the family because of my secret, I never felt that I completely belonged. There was the McNaught family and there was me, living on borrowed time until I was discovered.

The concept of not belonging to your family is a strange one for most heterosexual people, but a familiar one for most gay and lesbian people I know. A friend of mine suggested that being gay is like being an adopted child from a foreign country. In that situation, you often look and sound different from the rest of the family because of your physical characteristics or speech patterns. Thus, you might never trust that you truly fit in.

But here the comparison ends. Adopted children generally trust that they are wanted. Their parents accepted their uniqueness prior to adoption. The family with an adopted child is not likely to tolerate negative comments from others about the child's differences. Nor is the child's uniqueness a secret that must be kept from the family.

Initially I was terribly embarrassed by and afraid of my secret. I felt I was unworthy of my family's love, respect, and good reputation. And I was envious of my siblings, including Tommy, who I felt could talk openly and happily about their heterosexual lives.

Even after coming out to my family, I still felt that I didn't belong. Despite their thoroughly decent response to me, I experienced myself as being on probation when I was home. I felt vulnerable and I secretly worried that I must always be on my best behavior. Otherwise, I might be reminded of the pain and disappointment I was causing the family.

How much of my anxiety was caused by my heterosexism and homophobia and how much was due to my family's discomfort with the topic of homosexuality, I will never know for sure. I do know, though, that the more I came to accept my homosexuality as worthy of respect, the less tolerant I became of feeling vulnerable at home. The more I affirmed my homosexuality as my identity and not some unfortunate orientation, the less I felt I had in common with heterosexual siblings, cousins, nieces, and nephews. The more I valued my time with gay friends, the less interested I was in spending time in heterosexual family contexts.

"You've lost your sense of humor," I recall hearing. "You've changed." "You used to be so happy." "You've always spent your birthday with the family. Why not this year?"

As I matured into a less defensive posture and as various members of my family worked to better understand what it meant for me to be gay, I grew to feel more at ease with my heterosexual relatives. We began to spend more time together. We started to talk openly and casually about gay news stories, gay characters in television shows and movies, and friends they suspected might be gay. It was nice not to feel like such an outsider in my family.

"You've got your sense of humor back," I was told. "You seem happier."

Nevertheless, I never fully trusted that anyone in my family *really* understood my fears, joys, pain, or pride as a gay man. And I certainly never trusted that any of them could or would celebrate with me my sexual/emotional attractions.

While they might express regret about Harvey Milk's being assassinated, I was sure they wouldn't be up all night thinking about it. While they might laugh along with the play *La Cage aux Folles,* they wouldn't be bursting with excitement while listening to the song "I Am What I Am." While they might be concerned about AIDS, their hearts wouldn't ache constantly because of the friends who had died and will die.

Nor could I expect that when a handsome man appeared on television or walking down the beach, my heterosexual siblings or father would comment to me, "Hey, what do you think of him?"

Asking too much? Yet, I would occasionally hear, "Brian, look at that woman in the bikini. Are you honestly telling me that you aren't turned on by her?"

When I learned that I had a gay brother whom I liked and with whom I could communicate, my isolation in and alienation from the family ended. While I may never feel as if I truly belong at every family gathering, having a gay sibling provides me with the confidence that I'm no longer alone. Tommy not only gives me a link with my biological family but also truly understands my feelings as a gay man.

My brother and I find in each other a comfort similar, I imagine, to that available to compatible heterosexual siblings of the same sex. We feel safe with each other, sensing that we can discuss anything.

Tommy and I talk often, for instance, about issues from our childhood that we are currently working on in therapy. We're able to refine each other's memories and challenge each other's perceptions as no other person in our lives can.

"I don't remember that. How old was I when that happened?"

We also commiserate about our enormous fear of being discovered as gay in high school.

"Steve saw me staring at Dan Parks at the basketball game and just said, 'Stop it.' "

"He didn't say anything more?"

"Nope. Just 'Stop it.' "

And we laugh about our early same-sex crushes, sometimes on the same men.

"I used to stare at Dan Parks, too. Actually, his older brother Rich sat next to me in history. I *really* had a crush on him."

"Oh, me too."

Tom and I don't have to explain to each other why something is sad or funny. We can laugh together during a Lily Tomlin comedy sketch, shake our fists at the television when Pat Robertson appears, and hold hands and cry, as we did during Mom's funeral.

Tommy and I can also feign competition for the same male movie star or man on the street. "Dibs!"

We can expertly push each other's buttons. "See here, Skeezix!" we will say, recalling our father's diminutive.

"Stop it, Brian. I mean it!"

And we can take pride in each other's accomplishments as gay professionals.

Tom, for instance, was Congressman Gerry Studds's and Massachusetts Attorney General Jim Shannon's press secretary. He also was director of communications for the Bay State's AIDS Action Committee. I'm very proud of my gay brother!

When I was the mayor of Boston's liaison to the gay and lesbian community, Tom was on the mayor's staff in the survey research department. As two of only a handful of openly gay people in city hall at the time, we created the monumental "Boston Project," a landmark blueprint for government response to gay citizen needs. On the wall of my office is a signed photograph of us standing on either side of Mayor Kevin White.

Through all of our professional lives as gay men, Tom and I have been able to give each other the "that a boy!" encouragement and approval neither one of us was able to get from our father. Though we trusted that Dad loved us, we also knew he and Mom had preferred that we make gay civil rights our avocation and not our vocation.

"What exactly do I tell my friends that you do?" Mom lovingly asked with genuine concern.

"Got your book. Found it interesting. When are you going to write about something else?" Dad said.

"It's a great book. I'm real proud of you. People come up to me and say, 'Are you *the* Brian McNaught's brother?' " Tom says.

Ray enthusiastically welcomed Tommy into our home and into our lives. He encouraged our closeness and participated in it, laughing or crying with us during the retelling of our family stories. Ray also often expressed his envy at the gifts we got in having each other as gay brothers.

We all observed that there was no guarantee that gay siblings would necessarily get along or provide each other the wonderful support Tommy and I felt we had. One essential ingredient of our successful relationship was that we shared interests and values. One of the values we continue to share is a strong commitment to emotional healthiness.

Not long after Tom found his gay legs and his own apartment, Ray's brother David, the youngest of the seven boys, came to Boston from Kansas and moved into our guest room. David was a handsome, shiny-cheeked, corn-fed former college cheerleader in his early twenties who had lived his whole life with or near his parents in Wichita. Seven years younger than Ray, David was a "surprise" child.

At six-feet-two-inches tall, David charmed me instantly with his wonderful infectious laugh, his unabashed midwestern twang, and his childlike delight in the simple pleasures of life. And within a few days of his arrival, he secured my brotherly interest when he cautiously confirmed our suspicion that he too was gay.

Two weeks after David moved in, his folks arrived in Boston for a visit. Ray's parents were both raised on Kansas farms and are devout Catholics. They take particular pride in their eldest son, the missionary, and they are diehard fans of Notre Dame University and its sports teams.

When Ray came home from seminary at Notre Dame many years ago to tell his parents that he was gay, he was disowned and asked to leave the house. The family later reconciled, but Ray's homosexuality had yet to be fully accepted and our relationship had yet to be embraced. I, in fact, was often referred to by his mother as "what's his name." As a result, Ray distanced himself from the family, physically and emotionally.

On the first day of his parents' two-week visit to our home, I got a call at city hall from my friend Gerry (pronounced Gary) Studds. Years before, following the first Gay and Lesbian March on Washington, I had been introduced to Gerry at his Watergate apartment.

"Do you want to meet Gerry Studds at the Watergate?" my friend Billy Damon asked me after the march.

"Wow, the Watergate. Sure. But, who's Gerry Studds?" I asked.

"Who's Gerry Studds?" he repeated incredulously." He's the congressman who represents Cape Cod. He's brilliant. If Ted Kennedy was president, Studds would be Secretary of Interior."

"Oh," I said. "Is he gay?"

"Is he gay?" Billy said. "Don't ask that! Promise me that you won't ask him that. No one talks about that."

Gerry and I went to dinner that night and he confided in me that he was gay. Subsequently, Ray and I helped him come out. He started coming to our annual Christmas party, each year relaxing a little bit more. Now he called to say that he needed our help.

The congressman's home in Provincetown was surrounded by reporters demanding a comment on his pending censure by the House of Representatives for having had sex with a male page ten years earlier. Could he, Gerry asked, stay with us in our apartment on Beacon Street in Brookline? He needed a safe place to wait out the frenzy of media interest.

I explained to him that Ray's family was visiting but that of course he should come and we would all head to our cottage in New Hampshire the next morning.

I then called Ray at work to make sure his folks would be comfortable with our additional guest. He called me back to say his mother was in tears. Before Ray had the opportunity to ask her about Gerry joining us, she had asked, "Is David gay?"

"You need to ask David that," Ray responded.

"You've just answered my question," wept his mom.

When the subject of Gerry finally came up, she said she wasn't comfortable having him with us.

When I arrived home that evening, I found David in a back

bedroom, shutting his parents out with icy silence. "It's none of their business," he told me.

David's parents, sitting in the living room, were acting as if nothing had happened. "How are things at city hall?" his dad asked.

Ray paced back and forth in the kitchen, frustrated and embarrassed. "Why did they wait to bring this up on the first day of their vacation?" he asked. "And why won't David just tell them and get it over with?"

As I had not disinvited Gerry, Ray took his family to the cottage that evening. Our plan was to spend the weekend apart.

Gerry came into my bedroom in the middle of the night to alert me to the fire that was engulfing the back of the building next door. Smoke was pouring into our apartment. (The fire was intended to destroy the women's health clinic. That same clinic was terrorized several years later by an armed John Salvi, who murdered the receptionist.)

With the block now buzzing with firefighters and reporters, Gerry and I hid in the shadows until it was safe to reenter the apartment. The following morning, I called and asked Ray to prepare my in-laws for our arrival, as the smoke from the fire made our apartment unbearable.

I told Gerry nothing of the Struble family dynamics, except for the inquiries about David's sexuality. When we arrived in New Hampshire, we found David alone in the canoe in the middle of the lake, avoiding all questions from his parents. The national papers, which we bought on our way up to the cabin, were filled with reports on Gerry's refusal to apologize as had Representative Dan Crane for his activities with a female page.

Ray's dad, who called our guest "Senator" and "Jerry," wanted to know why he wouldn't apologize. Ray's mom periodically cried as she struggled with David's homosexuality and my name. An unexplained boat that drifted in front of the cottage for several hours raised the anxiety of everyone. Were they reporters?

Would Art and Mary Struble be photographed with Gerry Studds, and would the photograph appear in the hometown Wichita paper?

They weren't reporters, only people fishing, and Ray's folks survived the visit by the homosexual congressman and their youngest son's "don't ask, don't tell" strategy. Gerry survived the hounding of the press and the censure. Ray and I survived the two-week visit from the in-laws. And David, upon their departure, settled down and settled in for the next six months.

Like Tom when he first arrived, David was wrestling with the full implications of his homosexual feelings. Unlike Tom, he was the "baby" of the family who did not share a room or a lot of childhood memories with Ray.

"When I was in eighth grade, David was in kindergarten," Ray explained. "He used to hang around me during recess. Mom had to tell him to stop following me around and to make friends his own age."

Once again, David was young, vulnerable, and eager for the opportunity to get his bearings in the company of his older brother. This time around, the older brother wasn't calling in Mom to get the kid off his hands.

Yet, as was true with me regarding Tommy, Ray did have some reservations about David moving into his life. Part of his emergence into a comfortable gay identity required that he separate from his family and become emotionally self-reliant. Ray worried that having a younger sibling around who might still need family approval could threaten his detachment. David could trigger uncomfortable and unwanted emotional responses about family.

On the other hand, Ray loved his brother David. He also enjoyed feeling David's love of and admiration for him. Cautiously but deliberately they built a relationship of mutual trust and support. Ray and David became each other's link to and defense from the family. They learned to laugh together about the idiosyncracies of family members and to help each other when a conversation with a parent or sibling was unsettling.

And as was true for me with Tom, Ray was proud of David, of his good humor, his easygoing nature, and his loving heart. He enjoyed his company and the words of praise he heard about David from admiring friends. We both were proud gay big brothers.

Tommy and David met through us and are now best friends. They go dancing together nearly every weekend, as well as to movies and out to dinner. After Ray and I moved away from Boston, Tommy and David continued the tradition of getting together for each other's birthdays and Thanksgiving dinner and of exchanging Christmas gifts. When they travel with us, they share a hotel room. Ray and I have periodically suggested, somewhat seriously, that they be lovers. They laugh, say they aren't each other's type and that it would be like sleeping with your brother.

They are brothers and the four of us are a family, both of origin and of choice. We love one another and we care for one another. In each other's company we feel secure. None of us can imagine life without the four of us in it.

Ray, Tommy, David, and I often find ourselves side by side sitting at the funerals of our friends, marching during gay pride rallies, and walking silently through the displays of the AIDS Memorial Quilt.

We talk to each other on the phone at least once a week. We fax each other book reviews, AIDS updates, and Larson cartoons. Until my grandmother died at 101, we helped coordinate her birthday parties and Christmas Eve celebrations. We all have separate lives and separate friends but we thoroughly enjoy our time together. We share a passion for issues of social justice, for pistachios and skittles, for politics, for movies, for *The Simpsons*, and for gay pride.

In front of St. Peter's Basilica in Rome, David led us in the chant "Act up. Fight back. Fight AIDS." Later, Tommy saw me drop a note in the petitions box.

"What did it say?" he asked.

"Pray for the gay men and lesbian women who have been damaged by the rejection of the church," I answered.

"Cool!" he said as he pulled a piece of red ribbon from his wallet, cut off a piece and dropped it into the box.

"Where did that come from?" I asked.

"David and I went to the ACT UP rally at the last March on Washington. We were part of the group that surrounded the Capitol with a red ribbon. This is a piece of that," he said.

Thus began the family tradition of David and Tommy leaving signs of gay pride in the form of fragments of the red ribbon wherever we traveled. With great excitement and no small amount of ceremony they have pulled from Tom's wallet the sacred swatch and cut pieces for a rock in the Swiss Alps, a glacier in Juneau, the Notre-Dame de Paris belfry (which sounds its bells only on Bastille Day and when the pope visits), Oscar Wilde's tomb, the "Angels in America" (Bethesda) fountain in Central Park, and the dome of the Capitol in Washington, D.C.

Ray, David, Tom, and I feel secure together. In both heterosexual and homosexual crowds, no matter what the size, we know that we belong and are therefore generally shielded from the loneliness that one can feel in either crowd. When we travel, we don't do everything together—David and Tom, both being single, stay up later than Ray and I do—but when we are apart, we always trust there is a safe, welcoming group to which we can and will return.

On a cruise to Alaska, we sat as a family in the dining room. The ship's photographer, who roamed from table to table taking family photos, skipped our table. I tapped his back and said, "You *are* coming back here."

"Oh, sure if you want," he said, "but I didn't see any couples at the table."

"Wrong. They've been together eighteen years," piped in Tom and David as they proudly pointed to us.

"Where are all the women?" asked one matronly passenger who came to our table to satisfy her curiosity.

"We're gay," we responded.

"No, seriously," she insisted, "where are your wives?"

It's nice to be able to speak up to and laugh away such uncomfortable situations in the strong company of gay family.

We all fantasize about growing old together, yet we know there are no guarantees. David is HIV-positive, which makes us all very aware of how precious each moment together is. David is healthy and is energized by a positive attitude about living with HIV.

For the last few years we have traveled together on dream vacations, doing what we wanted when we wanted, driven by the desire to never say, "My one regret is that I never . . ."

One such dream realized was seeing Michelangelo's breathtaking statue of David in Florence. We four roamed independent of each other around this magnificent work of art. It is an incredible celebration of the male body, particularly poignant for us because of the sculptor's homosexuality.

We each smiled broadly as we circled the statue for detailed looks at the inspiring and erotic portrayal. We got giddy in the experience. I recalled for the group the cartoon caption from *Playboy*: "No, I said I would meet you under the big *clock!*" Tommy made us laugh by genuflecting in front of the statue. Ray, as always, took pictures—"Brian, go stand over there."

As I stood back to get another look, I noticed David talking with an elderly couple. After they walked away, he teared up. Ray noticed, walked over, heard what happened, and wrapped his arms around his brother as they cried quietly together. Tom and I kept a respectful distance until it appeared the moment had passed.

"David saw the old woman crying and asked if she was okay," Ray said as we were walking out. "Her husband explained that they had first viewed the statue twenty years ago. He was telling her to say 'goodbye.' She was crying because she knew they would never see it again."

"Well, we can all see it again if you want to come back next year," I said, foolishly hoping that Ray's and my finances could spare David the fear of death. "But maybe there are other places you would like to see."

"How about Vienna?" David asked with a big smile.

"Vienna sounds good to me," chimed in Tom as they laughed with delight and headed down the street arm in arm.

Two gay big brothers looked on with pride and felt twice-blessed.

7

About
Our Gay, Lesbian,
and Bisexual Youth

A few years ago, a letter arrived from a young gay high school student that I've carried in my briefcase ever since. It helps me not forget those we've left behind.

"I am sixteen years old, and a sophomore in high school," he wrote. "I know that you're a very busy man, so I'll try not to take up too much of your time.

"For the past three years I have been trying to find a way to tell my family and friends that I am a homosexual, but I am afraid to. You're the only person, other than my sex partner, that I have had the nerve to tell.

"When I first started having sex with my best friend three years ago, I thought it would only last until I had sex with a girl, but I was wrong. I had two sexual experiences with girls, but all I could think about was having anal intercourse with some handsome young guy, while I was with these girls.

"Some people might say I'm just too confused to understand, but I know that I am, as you say in your book *On Being Gay*, a constitutional homosexual, and I'm damn proud of it. The problem is that I want everyone else to know, but I've seen how the people at my school are treated if they're just suspected of being gay. How can I tell anyone how I feel?

"Another problem that I face is that the only person (guy) that I have had a semi-relationship with no longer lives here, and how am I supposed to find another lover when no one knows I'm gay?

"Most of the time I feel so lonely that I want to die. About a month ago, I felt so bad that I went into the bathroom and took thirty-two aspirin, forty-six sinus tablets, sixteen nasal decongestants, and eight amoxicillin tablets, but as you can see, it didn't work. When I went back in my room, all I could see was my mother crying at my funeral, so, crying and scared, I went and made myself vomit. I was sick for the rest of the week, but no one figured out why. Still every night I look at the .357 pistol in the dresser and think how easy it would be.

"I don't want to die. I just want a man that will love me and care for me, and let me love and care for him. God knows when that will be, but I keep trying to hold on, thinking that this will be the day.

"I don't know if anything in this letter makes sense, but I just needed to tell someone so that I wouldn't be alone so much. If you have time, I put a self-addressed stamped envelope in, in case you wanted to write me back.

"Thank you for writing *On Being Gay* and for being such an excellent guy.

"Mark Williams

"P.S. I asked our school librarian why the school library doesn't have a copy of [your books] *A Disturbed Peace* or *On Being Gay*. She said that certain parents don't want their children to read things like that. I told her I was going to write the principal an anonymous letter telling him how much help they had been for at least this gay kid, and if that didn't work, I'd write the school board and even the state board of education. I'll even send the money to pay for the books. That's my 'growl' for the day."

It is hard for me to imagine anyone reading this letter and not understanding the urgent need for an immediate and supportive response.

I quickly replied to Mark, of course, with praise, encouragement, and assurance of my interest. We corresponded for over a year, and I was grateful for the opportunity to ultimately have a positive impact on his life. But the .357 handgun in the bureau scared me. For the longest time I privately worried that my efforts would not be enough to deter him from picking it up out of loneliness.

Today, I continue to worry about the hundreds of thousands of his peers who are sometimes just barely surviving the isolation of their gay adolescence. They're invisibly coming of age in a more blatantly hostile world in which they're misunderstood, feared, and hated.

Sometimes the response of gay, lesbian, and bisexual youth to this socially sanctioned nightmare is to just give up, as Mark attempted to do. Thousands of gay kids make attempts on their lives every year. Many of them succeed.

Other gay, lesbian, and bisexual youth, in response to the siren song of adult gay liberation, cautiously step forward with quiet hope, only to be singled out for vicious reprisal.

Whose responsibility are these young gay people?

As a childless gay couple who pay federal, state, and local taxes, Ray and I believe that our public schools have a major share of the responsibility for the emotional and physical well-being of these youngsters. We feel strongly that, at the very least, our gay youth ought to feel safe at school. They ought to have access to a nonjudgmental counseling staff, a gay-literate administration and faculty, and current, supportive library resources. We also want them to get an affirming, inclusive education on human sexuality, and the opportunity to meet openly with others like themselves. Finally, we believe these young people, and their peers, need the role modeling provided by openly gay, lesbian, and bisexual faculty and staff.

But apparently that's not what most legislators, school boards, administrators, and teachers seem to have in mind. To begin with, many of them, remarkably enough, don't even see the problem. "What gay youth?"

If they do recognize the presence of young homosexual people in their schools, they often don't see as their task supporting the development of gay self-esteem. This is particularly true if they sense that their outreach will create any controversy.

Some, such as the former school board in Merrimac, New Hampshire, even go out of their way to make it more difficult for gay kids like Mark by barring from their schools any positive information on homosexuality. This includes library books, pamphlets in the guidance office, guest speakers and videos, and even discussion in class.

In Utah in 1996, the state legislature, in response to the heroic efforts of lesbian senior Kelli Peterson and friends to form a gay and straight alliance, passed a bill to ban gay clubs from all public high schools.

"Young people reach their teenage years and their sexuality starts developing. And I believe they can be led down that road to homosexuality," explained Utah Republican State Senator Craig Taylor, the bill's sponsor.[1]

"Free speech does not include recruiting them into a homosexual lifestyle that can kill them," stated Republican State Representative David Bresnahan, who, ironically, had a gay brother who died of AIDS.[2]

Yet, it wasn't a homosexual "lifestyle" that nearly killed Jamie Nabozny, a former student in the Ashland, Wisconsin, school district. It was the unchecked behavior of bullying classmates who, according to his successful suit against the school[3], kicked, punched, shoved, and urinated upon him; their attacks led to internal bleeding, surgery, two unsuccessful suicide attempts, and ultimately his dropping out of school.

The Ashland School District doesn't dispute the allegations. It all happened as described. But, they insist, they are not responsible for the actions of one student toward another.[4]

Then who is?

The Commonwealth of Massachusetts agrees that their schools *are* responsible for the well-being of gay, lesbian, and bisexual students. In response to the intensive lobbying efforts of hundreds of gay youth, as well as by their adult supporters, model legislation was passed and signed into law by Republican Governor William Weld in December 1993. H3353 reads:

> No person shall be excluded from or discriminated against in admission to a public school of any town, or in obtaining the advantages, privileges, and courses of study of such public school education on account of race, color, sex, religion, national origin, or sexual orientation.[5]

In response to this law, a program entitled "Safe Schools for Gay and Lesbian Students" was created by the state department of education to guide and monitor the progress of the state. Teachers, counselors, and administrators began seeking better education on gay issues. Schools started ordering extensive resources on homosexuality for their libraries. And gay, lesbian, and bisexual faculty began coming out in greater numbers.

The San Francisco United School District has also addressed the issue by creating Support Services for Gay and Lesbian Youth. Their sixty thousand students receive "age-appropriate" education about homosexuality, and "gay sensitive" adults have been designated as counselors in both middle and high schools. Similar efforts have been initiated in St. Paul and in Los Angeles, inspired by the trailblazing efforts of Virginia Uribe and her Project 10.

But that's not much good to Mark in Enid, Oklahoma, or

Jamie in Ashland. What about them and their peers throughout the country who, in the words of one gay youth, "cower in their closets?"

Kevin Jennings, the inspiring founder and executive director of the Gay, Lesbian, and Straight Teachers Network (GLSTN), helped coordinate the Massachusetts effort and wants to see similar legislation and results across the country. But he's a realist.

"We'd love to see every state legislature pass such a law," he told me. "But it's mostly only going to happen one school at a time. Our goal at GLSTN is to get one teacher, one counselor, one principal, or one school board member to understand the issue and to start the effort to improve the environment. Such changes of heart and mind at the local level will eventually lead to statewide policy changes."

The most effective tool GLSTN has to create such change, he says, is when we adult gay, lesbian, and bisexual people who struggled with our homosexuality as youths write our high school principals, teachers, counselors, or coaches to let them know what our lives were like when we were teens, and what good or bad things were done for or to us. Also, he urges, we need to ask what is being done today to support gay youth.

"The effect is amazing," Kevin said. "We're now getting calls from school counselors and principals asking for help because they received a letter from a former gay student. They tell us they had no idea how bad the situation was or how important a teacher or coach's outreach had been."

If most gay, lesbian, and bisexual adults are like Ray and me, they feel pretty disenfranchised from their high schools and have bittersweet recollections of their time there. We rarely read anything but the "In Memoriam" sections of our alumni newsletters and neither of us has contributed money to our alma mater. It feels like a time and place best left behind.

The trouble is, there are gay, lesbian, and bisexual kids in those schools whom we are also leaving behind.

Inspired by GLSTN's Back to School program, I sent copies of my books and gay educational videos to the principal of Brother Rice High School in Birmingham, Michigan, for its library. I also offered to speak to the faculty and students, and requested to meet with the counseling staff. Though we have yet to come up with a mutually agreeable date, I believe they are genuinely interested in talking and that it will eventually happen.

Regrettably, the teacher to whom I would like to have written died recently, denying me the opportunity to say "thank you" for the one lifeline that was thrown my way in my four years at the all-boys Catholic prep school.

Brother Jerry Markert began our senior honors English class one day by displaying a male porn magazine. Holding up the cover for all of us to see, he explained that he had received the unsolicited magazine in the mail and thought we young men should know such things exist.

You can imagine the laughter, derision, moving of desks, and fake vomiting that greeted his efforts. Yet, I have only the faintest recollection of what was happening around me. All I can recall is the cover, as clear in my mind today as if I had looked at it this morning rather than thirty years ago.

A handsome, muscled, naked, dark-haired man stood on large rocks, his left foot resting up a level from his right. The sky was bright blue. Green foliage framed the scene. And an unwelcome large, bright yellow star blocked the view of his genitals.

I shudder now to think of how I would have responded had anyone noticed how intensely I viewed every detail of that picture. "Look at McNaught! He likes it! He's *queer*, Brother. McNaught's a *queer!*"

If any classmates did notice my expressionless stare, they didn't say so. And if they did, I didn't hear them. I was too scared, too excited, and too hungry for more. Though riddled with guilt and shame, I felt obsessed.

Brother Markert had unknowingly spoken my secret language. The man on his magazine cover had reached out and embraced me as no one else in my life had before. For the briefest moment,

I left the familiar but terribly uncomfortable world of my peers and was pulled into a yet unknown but very welcoming place of my own kind.

As I reluctantly refocused, I became more conscious of the laughter and banter. I took on protective cover by joining in the "fun," but I felt terribly alone. I feared that if I dared tell them of my feelings, they would pretend to vomit around me.

That evening, I anxiously paced around the house, desperate to communicate with someone what I had felt that day. There was only one person I could think to call. Brother Markert. He knew about this world, even if he didn't belong to it. I trusted by the nonjudgmental manner in which he had raised the issue in class that he wouldn't make fun of me.

It felt like an eternity before my younger sister, Maureen, freed up the phone by ending her interminable conversation with her thirteen-year-old friend. Then I had to wait a second lifetime as Brother Markert made his way to the telephone in the monastery.

"I was wondering if I could talk to you tomorrow after school," I asked. "I was really upset by the magazine you showed us in class today."

Though smoking was prohibited on school grounds, Brother allowed me to chain-smoke through our hour-and-a-half meeting, during which I ducked and swayed and danced around the subject of my homosexuality.

"I think I'm bisexual," I finally blurted out. "I like girls, of course. You know Jody. She and I will probably get married. But I had this funny reaction to the magazine you showed us and I don't know how to talk about it."

I was so nervous, I don't recall exactly what Brother Markert said to me, other than I should not worry about my feelings. "They are normal for a boy your age."

Brother Markert didn't tell me all of the things I now think a young gay high school student needs to hear, but he was accessible and nonjudgmental, and he provided me the only safe opportunity I had ever received to raise the issue. Furthermore, he assured me that I was *normal!* For those reasons, he will always have a very special place in my heart. (So too will the man on the front cover of that pornographic magazine.)

GLSTN hopes that if gay, lesbian, and bisexual adults write to their Brother Markerts, more and more teachers and counselors will start thinking of ways to create bridges for their gay, lesbian, and bisexual students to identify their special needs. Even if we no longer know the faculty at our high school, a letter to the principal or the guidance department could make a big difference. It seems like such an easy thing for us to do in our attempt to stop the awful loneliness and fear experienced by those like Mark, Jamie, and Kelli we have left behind.

Until our schools finally do take steps to protect our gay youth from isolation, harassment, and desperation, and initiate programs of support, these youngsters are left to fend for themselves and to rely on whatever assistance is available outside of school. Fortunately, there are some people who have stepped forward to help create a few safety nets for them.

Michael May is one such person. He's a Michigan real estate manager by trade, and a coach and youth worker by passion. Had Mark lived in Grand Rapids instead of Enid, I would have immediately sent him into Michael's welcoming arms.

Michael was thirty-eight years old when he was approached, in 1984, by quiet and shy nineteen-year-old Sean, who wanted help in starting a gay youth group.

"The people at P-FLAG (Parents, Families and Friends of Lesbians and Gays) sent him to me," explained Michael. "I was doing youth work at Fountain Street Church and they didn't know where else to send him."

Sean had attended meetings for gay Christians and those of the local women's group but was frustrated by their lack of resources for gay youth. He wanted something like the organization he had attended back in Portland, called Windfire.

Michael acknowledged that he had no idea how to locate other gay youth to join the new group, but he promised Sean that he would work with him to form a local Windfire.

"I'll meet with you every Thursday night at the church, even if it's just the two of us," he told him. "You have my word."

For three weeks, it *was* just the two of them that met. And for the first nine to twelve months, there were just three or four in attendance. Nevertheless, Michael showed up as promised every Thursday evening.

"We decided right off the bat that the meetings were going to be positive," Michael explained. "We didn't want it to be a gripe session during which everyone complained how horrible it was to be gay. Everyone was expected to give their first name and tell one positive thing that had happened to them during the week. It could even be about a movie they'd seen. When someone would say that nothing positive had happened, I'd say, 'Okay, of all the *horrible* things that happened, what was the least horrible?' "

The kids agreed with the need to focus on the positive, but eventually convinced Michael they needed at least five minutes at each meeting to vent about how hard they found it that week to be a gay, lesbian, bisexual, or transgender teenager.

After the introductions, Michael helped coordinate an activity to get a discussion going. He might introduce an icebreaker that he had used with other teen groups, bring in an outside speaker, show an educational video, or even take the kids on an outing, like bowling.

At the end of the evening, he always offered them a little bit of gay history, usually by reading off the birthdays of well-known gay people and discussing the contributions these women and men had made to the movement and to society.

Between meetings, on more than one occasion, Michael had the kids to his home to swim and took them out on his boat. They even made a trip together to Detroit for the annual Gay Pride parade and rally.

"What they needed most was a place in which they could feel safe to be themselves and to have open conversations," he explained. "Our criterion was that we always wanted to do things with which even the most timid would feel comfortable."

Eventually the group grew to twenty young people, aged fourteen to twenty-two. That includes those who would sit outside the room week after week and just listen.

Timmy was initially such a visitor.

"He was a fourteen-year-old from a small school," explained Michael. "For three weeks he sat in the hall and wouldn't come in. Thirty percent of the time, there's a kid outside in the hall just listening.

"We leave them alone," he said. "If you go out and try to coax them in, they can be frightened away. It's best to let them come in at their own pace."

Eventually Timmy did, but for several meetings he wouldn't look up at the group.

"He was the kid without a face," Michael recalled. "You never saw it. I used to look over, though, and occasionally see his tears hitting his hands.

"But you should see him now," he added with excitement. "He's smiling. Interacting. He's a whole different person."

So too is Sondra. She's another of this group's "100-plus" success stories.

By Michael's description, Sondra was a 200-plus-pound, timid, embarrassed, fifteen-year-old black girl whose mother called her "queer" and "dyke" rather than by name.

"She's still a little shy," Michael said, "but you should see Sondra now. She lost all of the excess weight, she's very attractive, and she graduated with honors from high school. She told us that when she joined the group, she had wanted to kill herself. She credits the group with saving her life."

Michael and members of the group have helped spawn a half-dozen other Windfires throughout the state. He also regularly meets with human services professionals, counselors, teachers, and probation officers to explain the needs of gay youth and to inform them of Windfire's services.

Michael feels that there are four things gay adults need to do for gay, lesbian, and bisexual youth:

- Mentor. "They need guidance. It's easy to volunteer."
- Be role models. "They need someone to look up to, to admire, to want to be like."
- Provide financial support for youth programs. "Our numbers ebb and flow according to our ability to advertise our services. When we run out of money, we can't get the word out that we're there for them."
- Sit down with school counselors and teachers. "I tell them, 'I don't care how you feel about the subject, you've *got* to deal with this. You can't impose your values on the kids.' "

Though Michael is still very involved in Windfire, he no longer facilitates the group. He's delighted to say he was able to find a gay man and a lesbian woman to take over.

"The kids need those positive role models," he said.

Yes, Michael May is heterosexual, but he hates having people know.

"I can't stand hearing someone say, 'I'm supportive but I'm straight,' " he explained. "Why do people need to say that?"

Michael is the long-term "significant other" of my buddy, Jan Lunquist, director of education for Planned Parenthood in Grand Rapids. She never held a title in Windfire, but she too opened up her heart and home to the gay, lesbian, and bisexual youth, filled out grant applications, put Michael in touch with people who could be helpful, and provided gay-positive sexuality education to the kids. She's also on the front lines of the battle, educating administrators, teachers, and counselors to their responsibility to gay youth.

None of this has been done without a price tag, of course. Michael and Jan have received threatening letters and calls because of their efforts. But they're undaunted.

Employing Michael's meeting format, I have some positive things to report about the status of gay and lesbian youth today.

In the words of Kevin Jennings, there is now a "phenomenal proliferation of gay youth groups." Most have resulted from the initiatives taken by gay youths like Sean.

Now when I hear from young people like Mark, I'm able to immediately direct them to the Internet, where they can access the ever-growing list of local gay youth resources (by entering *http://www.outproud.org/outproud/*) or materials for fighting homophobia in their schools *(http://www.glstn.org/freedom/)*. In addition, I give them two toll-free numbers, both of which provide information on national and local resources. The Indianapolis Youth Group can be reached at 1-800-347-TEEN and Out Youth in Austin at 1-800-96-YOUTH. Finally, the Hetrick-Martin Institute in New York, one of the pioneers in gay youth work, also has a list of resources in their publication *You Are Not Alone*.

More good news to report is that an increasing number of gay youth today have a healthy sense of entitlement and more gay adults are responding to the issue with less fear.

"When I was at Concord Academy, I taught an independent study course on gay history," Kevin told me. "I had two lesbian seniors in the fall of '94. I was discussing oppression, and Sally said, 'Why don't gay people just run for office and do something about it?'

"I explained about how internalized homophobia made a lot of gay people feel as if they couldn't run and win. So Sally said, 'Well, then *I'll* just run for office!'

"Here was a seventeen-year-old girl who felt entitled to equal treatment and who was not afraid to do things for herself," he said. "How different they are from the way you and I were at their age. Studies are showing that gay youth are naming themselves earlier and earlier. Our generation knew we were different but we didn't know the word.

"Another way they are different is that they want and expect to do normal teen things, like go to the prom," Kevin continued. "We cut ourselves off from typical teenage things. We either didn't go to the prom or took a date we didn't want to be with. They want to do what other kids do, but in their own way."

Gay adults are different today too, he observed.

"There was a time when gay men, in particular, would make an inappropriate comment when they heard I worked with gay youth," Kevin said. "That doesn't happen much anymore. The community seems more grown-up about the issue. Gay adults are realizing that gay, lesbian, and bisexual youth are our responsiblity.

"We're all changing the concept of community," he offered. "We're understanding that *real* communities span generations. They involve our elders and our youth. We're also realizing that when we reach out to gay youth, we do some important healing with our own 'wounded child' issues."

(He's right. After I contacted my high school principal and received word from him that he appreciated receiving my books and tapes, I felt considerably less alienated from my high school. A door was opened to possibly reclaim an important period of my life that I have sometimes bitterly resented.)

One last bit of good news to report is the emergence of heterosexual high school and college students as allies and advocates of gay youth. Given the opportunity to learn of the oppression that their gay, lesbian, and bisexual classmates face, many students react with powerful signs of support.

"They're outraged, horrified!" said Kevin in describing the reaction of straight high school students to his presentation on growing up gay. "They understand that it is an issue of *fairness*."

So too do many of the college students to whom I have spoken. At the College of the Holy Cross in Worcester, Massachusetts, for instance, an "Allies" group of gay and straight students was formed immediately after my talk and continues to thrive.

"The support group has grown so large that [we] had to move it to another location," wrote Kim McElaney, director of the college chaplains, in a letter to me updating the changes on campus. "Every kind of education or training program that exists here at the College to address issues of diversity, violence, prejudice, stereotypes, etc., always includes homophobia and issues pertaining to gays, lesbians, and bisexuals."

Now to the five minutes of bad news.

Most gay kids today are not as self-affirmed as Kelli, Sean, and Sally. In fact, they're probably just as frightened and alienated as—if less confused than—I was in Brother Markert's classroom. And because of all of the publicity about gay issues generated by gay adults, homophobic teenagers are now more agitated about the subject than were my peers. They're also more clever in identifying who might be gay, lesbian, or bisexual. I can't imagine not being pegged by today's television- and film-savvy young adults had they seen me mentally drift off to the rocks to join my naked new male friend in senior honors English class.

Furthermore, while there's an abundance of healthy gay youth groups now available, they are *not* a substitute for what must happen in schools, and most gay and lesbian young people will never find or use them. Youth groups are a wonderful lifeline for some kids, and their existence and growth must be supported personally and financially, but they are not the long-term solution to the problem. The schools must be.

The worst and most alarming news yet to report is that those people who oppose fair and equal treatment for gay, lesbian, and bisexual youth in our public schools have entered the discussion in a Trojan horse called "parental rights."

Because many people have come to see outright bans on gay-positive information as blatantly bigoted, tactics are changing. The aim of "parental rights" legislation is to effect the same goal by putting control of what is taught in public schools into the hands of disgruntled parents.

"It sounds innocuous enough," explained Kevin. "Who could object to parents' being involved in what their children are taught? But these bills that are popping up at the local and state level enable individual parents to dictate not only what *their* children are taught but what *all* children are taught.

"It's the meanest, dirtiest trick in the book," he said. "The easiest way to panic a society is to say something is a threat to their children. What the sponsors of these bills want is complete control of what is taught, who teaches it, and what resources are available to the students."

But public schools don't belong to a handful of unhappy parents alone. Public schools are funded by the community through taxes to serve the entire community. The schools also belong to us to serve *our* children.

Anthropologist Margaret Mead once observed that people without children may feel no sense of investment in the future. But she wasn't talking about me or any other gay, lesbian or bisexual adults I know. We all *do have* children. Their names include Mark, Kelli, Jamie, Sean, Timmy, Sondra, and Sally.

We may not have given them physical birth, but they are ours to watch over until their own parents understand and accept the responsibility to protect and nurture them. Furthermore, these gay, lesbian, and bisexual youths *know* they are our children. They write us secret letters, make anonymous calls, or send untraceable Internet messages to report their sexual awakening and their need for guidance.

Our gay children watch us from a distance as we make our adult way in the world, and they want to follow. They want to come out, to claim our name as their own, and to join our community. But they are afraid and they need our help.

Our gay, lesbian, and bisexual youth are our future. The growth and strength of our community depends upon their survival and emotional well-being. We must be invested in them. We can't leave them behind.

That means stopping the Trojan horse of "parental rights" by showing up at a school board meeting or a candidate's night to claim the rights of *our children* to a bias-free education and a safe and productive learning environment.

"I am concerned," we can rightfully say, "about how our gay, lesbian, and bisexual youth are being treated in our public schools. What programs are in place for them? What books are available to them?"

We can also donate appropriate books to the school library, offer to meet with the counseling staff, write the "Back to School" letter to the principal or our favorite teacher, financially support the gay youth group, and mentor those who hunger for adult role models. For other suggestions or for guidance in our efforts, we can call GLSTN in New York City at (212) 727-0135.

An African proverb reminds us that "it takes an entire village to raise a child." When the child is gay, lesbian, or bisexual, this is particularly true.

Hang in there kids, we won't let you down!

8

ABOUT
OUR ALLIES

The donation card explains that if Ray and I give X amount of money to the organization we will be "Angels." If we give half as much, they'll think of us as "Benefactors."

For half as much money as that, we can be "Patrons." If not patrons, we can still be "Supporters," and if not that, we can make a minimum donation and sneak in as "Friends."

To tell you the truth, though, we're not the least bit influenced in our giving by the title conferred upon us by the organization's marketing strategists. We decide how much we want to commit to a cause financially and then let the group grade our contribution.

I believe the same is true for most heterosexual women and

men who involve themselves in the civil rights struggle of gay, lesbian, and bisexual people. They don't lend their support in order to get a title. They respond at the level at which they feel most comfortable being invested.

My kid sister Maureen, for instance, quizzed the pastors of the neighboring churches about their position on homosexuality, as she searched for a place to worship with her two young boys.

"You see, my two brothers are gay and I don't want to feel any conflict between my church family and my real family," she explained to them.

I was real proud to hear of her efforts, particularly given her previous involvement in a fundamentalist church. But she didn't interview the pastors to make me proud. She did it because she felt it was the right thing for her to do.

That's what motivates most people to speak up, to stand up, and, if you will, to cough up in support of the issue. They join the battle for gay rights because they feel it's the right thing to do. Why they care, and the degree to which they do, are other matters.

Most gay men and women know some straight people who support them, and who are doing what they can to make the world a safer, saner place for them. Sometimes all these heterosexuals can do is simply not laugh at a "fag" or "dyke" joke. Sometimes, they choose to do much, much more.

There are many such people in my world. And whether they know it or not, their caring efforts touch my life deeply. They continually reassure me that I'm loved and not alone. That's very important for everyone to feel.

The image of my older sister, Kathy, for example, crying as she stood with gay people around her, applauding me at the end of one of my public talks on homosexuality will comfort me until the day I die.

The words of my sister-in-law, Judy, to her fundamentalist housekeeper also bolster my sometimes diminished spirits. "I have two gay brothers," she said. "I love them very much, and I won't hear anything negative about homosexuality."

I'm keenly and gratefully aware of similar responses from several other members of my big, extended family.

My mother's cousin, Sister Marcella, for instance, was an invaluable source of encouragement and stability to my parents and to me when I came out publicly. "He's the same wonderful boy you've always loved," she would remind them.

During my civil rights struggle with the church, my cousins Kathleen and Patty surprised me with proud letters of support. And my cousin Ginny now keeps me up to date on the close friendship she and her boys have with the male couple who live next door. Most recently, my niece Amy excitedly told me of her efforts to have me speak on her campus. "People need to hear what you have to say," she declared.

Perhaps the most unexpected and, in my eyes, one of the most courageous displays of support came from my cousin Meredith's young daughter, Becka, a junior at the time in a small high school in very rural Maine.

In response to an advanced English class assignment to write a biography, she asked me if I would consent to be her subject. She thought it was "cool" that a relative of hers had written a book, produced a video, and gave speeches on homosexuality.

Becka's bold gesture in itself was extraordinarily impressive to me, particularly given the teasing she took from some uncomfortable classmates, who themselves had chosen to chronicle the lives of their grandparents. But far more touching to me was her invitation to join the subjects of the other student biographies for a special reception in the school's library.

One by one her peers stood to read selections from their essays. Their grandparents filled the first row of chairs, arranged in a semicircle around the table laden with cookies and punch. One by one, "Gram" or "Gramps" self-consciously stood, and, amid hearty applause, joined her or his biographer to pose for the Kodak-toting English teacher. Faces beamed with pride.

"*The Life of Brian,*" Becka announced in a loud, steady voice, capturing the attention of the room. "Brian Robert McNaught is an expert on homosexuality and speaks at colleges and businesses across the country. . . . Brian lives with his partner, Ray Struble, and their yellow lab, Brit. . . . Brian's work is important to society because we need to know more about homosexuals in order to lessen prejudice and reduce misconceptions."

Polite applause by the other students and the somewhat startled honorees accompanied me as I joined Becka for our photograph by the broadly smiling instructor. A copy of her biography, which includes a picture of Ray and me, is now on the shelves of the school's library. The original is among my treasured possessions.

Such amazing, unsolicited support challenges both my gnawing fear that I have nothing in common with my "embarrassed" heterosexual family and my defensive posturing that I'm completely self-reliant, not needing anything from anybody. When individual family members reach out, I'm reminded how very important they are to me, and how much I want their interest in and encouragement of my life and work.

Like most gay, lesbian, and bisexual people I know, I also want to feel that I belong in the larger family of humans, and I consciously look for indications that I'm understood and appreciated by heterosexuals. Many days it's a frustrating, lonely search, but sometimes I'm delightfully taken by surprise by the source and degree of this support.

When, for instance, Ray and I lived in Gloucester, Massachusetts, a charming Italian-Portuguese fishing community north of Boston, we displayed the rainbow flag in front of our home, and greeted our arriving gay, lesbian, and bisexual friends with hugs and kisses in the driveway. But we never had "the conversation" about being gay with our neighbors.

Across the street from us lived a retired city official named Bill Cafasso. On one side of him was Laura Hersey, the eighty-year-old widow of a popular minister. On the other was a former Navy commander, Bud McKinnon, and his wife, Mildred.

Two or three times a week, I would stop by Laura's home to see if she wanted to join me for a walk on the beach. On one such outing, she offered: "I heard you on radio last night." (I was interviewed on the decision of then-Governor Michael Dukakis to bar gay people from being foster parents.)

"So, what did you think?" I asked.

"I thought you did real good," she answered.

"Thanks," I said, "but what do you think about the issue?"

"I think people ought to be left alone," she said. "It's nobody's business what others do in private. Besides, I don't know what it has to do with their ability to be good foster parents."

It was wonderful to hear and very important to me to learn that I had a neighbor who was so supportive on gay issues. It put a good-sized chink in my us-versus-them armor, and enabled Ray and me to feel much less like outsiders.

Then, a couple of days after the local bookstore put a copy of *On Being Gay* in the front window, Bill came into the driveway where I was playing with Brit.

"Hey, I saw your book in the bookstore," he said.

"Oh yeah?" I said, caught a bit off guard.

"Yeah, and I bought it," he continued.

"Oh yeah?" I answered, realizing this conversation had an intended direction.

"Yeah," he said, "and I learned something about you that I didn't know."

"What's that?" I asked.

"You're Irish!" he laughed as he winked and drove out the driveway.

The next night, the Commander called.

"McKinnon here," he announced.

"Hi Bud, how are you doing?" I asked.

"I didn't know we had a Hemingway in the neighborhood," he said, ignoring my question.

"Oh, the book," I answered.

"Yeah," he said, "Cafasso told me you've got a book out. Well, I'm going to get a copy."

"Great," I said, not sure he knew what the book was about.

After a few seconds of awkward silence he continued.

"Listen son, let me tell you why I'm calling. You know that I spent the better part of my life on the battlefield. And I'm damn proud of that. But the way I figure it, everyone's got to go to battle in their lifetime, and I want you to know that the wife and I are proud of you."

A few years later, as Ray and I prepared for a career-motivated move out of the state, the same no-nonsense man was confronted at a chamber of commerce meeting by someone who menacingly inquired about the "boys."

"Best damn neighbors I've ever had," Bud responded.

Though Ray and I have relocated three times since, we never will forget, nor fail to appreciate, our neighbors in Gloucester.

The track coach at my high school has also left on me a life-long impression.

Reportedly, when I came out publicly in *The Detroit News* in 1974, my name was removed from the Christian Leadership Award plaque that hung on the wall outside the principal's office. Bob Stark, two years ahead of me at Brother Rice High School and now on the faculty, apparently spent his own money to have a new name tag made up. He then personally screwed it back onto the plaque.

As the story was told to me, it was removed again. Bob then had another made up and let it be known that he would continue to do so. As a result, my name has remained on the award roster.

His determined response to such mean-spiritedness touched

not only my life but undoubtedly that of every gay student who watched in amazed silence as the drama unfolded.

What do we call such people? How do we categorize their investment in fair treatment for gay men and women? We know that they don't speak up to gain a title, but we'd like to be able to call them something that designates the special status they have in our hearts and in our movement.

At the very least, I consider any heterosexual who is more positive than neutral on the subject of gay civil rights—particularly given the current social climate of intolerance—to be a *Friend* of the cause. In this country today, millions of Americans qualify for the title.

Friends are the women and men who feel it's wrong to discriminate against or harass people because they're gay. These are the individuals who, at a minimum, don't laugh at or tell anti-gay jokes. They also don't casually use the words "fag," "dyke," "homo," or "queer" as put-downs. And they don't turn off or away from thoughtful, positive portrayals or discussions of gay people, though they may not seek them out.

Unlike many of their associates, who are often what I think of as "unconsciously incompetent" on the issue of homosexuality, Friends are aware of how maliciously and hurtfully gay people are talked about and treated. These men and women would therefore not knowingly be mean to a suspected or openly gay young person or adult. They may even have a gay, lesbian, or bisexual friend.

Among the heterosexuals who support gay people, Friends make up the largest category. They're the often silent majority whose numbers are known only when Gallup takes a poll. Currently, they're the majority of Americans who are opposed to discrimination against homosexuals on the job but are not yet ready to support openly gay people serving in the military or the idea of gay marriage.

Friends generally consider themselves to be "social moderates." They tend to see homosexuality as a behavior that is separate from the person. They tolerate the behavior, but love or respect the individual. Thus, they often view the civil rights struggle of gay people as distinct from those struggles based on race, gender, and other "intrinsic" differences.

Friends tend to be reactive rather than proactive. They may be dating or married to someone who is anti-gay, or may belong to an organization or church that is hostile to homosexuals. If so, they withhold support of, and may even challenge, homophobic words and deeds. On the other hand, they value these relationships and don't see such anti-gay behavior as grounds for losing friends or status.

Nor are these heterosexual women and men likely to respond positively to pro-gay efforts. Friends endorse treating gay people with decency but aren't yet invested enough in the issue to go out of their way to be supportive. For instance, they feel it was wrong for the Cracker Barrel restaurant chain to have fired eleven gay people without cause,[1] but they probably would eat there anyway. They don't see the personal advantage in being more involved, so they make the minimum contribution necessary to feel that they're doing the right thing.

I can think of many people I would put into the category of Friends, including some family members, high school and college classmates, lots of church and business leaders, and many politicians.

I'm very grateful for the supportive positions taken by Friends on behalf of gay people. Their vote has often been the deciding factor in referendums on gay civil rights. And I believe that as they come to better understand the impact of gay oppression and how it conflicts with their basic values, their investment in ensuring the equal treatment of gay people will deepen.

If so, they might well become what I call *Allies* of the gay community. The distinguishing characteristics of Allies are that they're "consciously competent" about gay, lesbian, and bisexual issues and are decidedly proactive.

These heterosexual women and men educate themselves

about gay issues. They go out of their way to learn more by reading books, going to films, attending lectures, and participating in community events, such as the viewing of the AIDS quilt. Allies also might join support groups in high school and college, and later look for a local chapter of P-FLAG (Parents, Families and Friends of Lesbians and Gays) or GLSTN (Gay, Lesbian, and Straight Teachers Network). And they would certainly avoid eating at a Cracker Barrel restaurant.

While conscious of the thinking of their nonsupportive straight friends, heterosexual Allies equally value the opinion of gay women and men. They may continue to view their own orientation as the preferred norm, but they see homosexuality as intrinsic to the being of gay and lesbian people, just like race and gender. Thus, they give heterosexism and homophobia the same weight that they give racism and sexism.

Allies can be counted upon to speak up and protest anti-gay behavior even when there are no gay people present. They're not uncomfortable with their commitment to the cause, though in truth they'd prefer that others not think of them as gay.

Heterosexual Allies, who might describe themselves as "social liberals," see how their own lives are enriched by their pro-gay activities, so they donate more of themselves than the minimum that's required.

The consistent support of our political, religious, and professional Allies is what keeps the gay liberation movement mainstream. Without the investment of heterosexual people of all ages, races, and religious beliefs educating their family members, friends, and neighbors, writing letters to the editor, calling in to talk shows, and faxing messages to their legislators, gay people would feel completely disenfranchised, and those who desperately seek to set back the clock on our civil rights struggle would triumph.

Among these important Allies are individuals who eventually make an even deeper connection with and commitment to gay, lesbian, and bisexual people. These heterosexual men and women find themselves so in tune with our concerns that they could be described as being "unconsciously competent." For them, homosexuality, bisexuality, and heterosexuality are points on a single continuum, with each serving a purpose and none being better than the others.

In their minds, gay rights are human rights, no more, no less, and impossible to compromise. And they're aware of and uncomfortable with the excluding nature of their heterosexual privileges, such as the freedom to safely express affection in public.

These individuals see gay, lesbian, and bisexual people not only as fellow human beings who need a helping hand, but also as beautifully unique and gifted creatures who have important insights to offer them and the rest of straight society.

Such a person is more than an Ally. In my mind, he or she has become an *Advocate* who takes actions because they're the right thing to do regardless of what others, heterosexual or homosexual, may think.

Straight Advocates are often dismissed by hostile observers as having a secret agenda. In truth, they can be so knowledgeable about and comfortable with the issues that even their gay and lesbian friends forget that they're heterosexual.

But these women and men don't care what others assume about their sexual orientation. They're flattered rather than threatened when they learn a person of the same gender finds them attractive. And it's precisely this self-confident lack of concern that frees them to do their important work.

Advocates take the initiative. For instance, they form groups to fill a need, petition their professional associations to take a stand, donate money to the full extent of their means, and, yes, picket outside of the Cracker Barrel restaurant to make their point. Such men and women are prime examples of the attitude, "If not me, who? If not now, when?"

Advocates might describe themselves as "socially progressive." The gay cause is their cause and they don't care who knows it.

Sometimes, our Advocates are forced to decide between their advocacy and their livelihood, their reputation, or perhaps even their safety. Their efforts on behalf of gay people are seen as such a threat that the opposition will do anything to stop them.

When Advocates commit themselves so much to the cause of gay liberation that they abandon themselves at a cost most others would be unwilling to pay, I call them *Heroes*.

President John F. Kennedy wrote about such Heroes in his book *Profiles in Courage*.[2] They're women and men who though not seeking martyrdom do not run away from it. Given the choice, they'd prefer to be left alone to do their work, but personalities and events confront them with unavoidable choices.

There's no political designation for such people, nor a race, gender, religious affiliation, or age that is predictable. Heroes of the gay community come from all walks of life.

I recently made a list of all of the straight people in my life whom I recalled as being supportive of me as a gay man, directly or indirectly. While I'm sure I overlooked some names—and I know that there are people missing because I'm unaware of their advocacy—I was nevertheless impressed with the incredible scope and length of my list.

I then assigned each name a label: Friend, Ally, Advocate, or Hero.

The names came from high school and college days, from the workplace, the Church, and the neighborhood. They came from family and friends, from college campuses at which I've spoken, organizations to which I belong, and letters and phone calls that I've received.

Then I expanded the list to include those whom I've never met but whose good words or deeds have touched my life as a gay man. Those names came from government, religious institutions, the business world, television, radio, the silver screen, news stories and op-ed pages, museums, concert halls, Broadway stages, libraries, and art galleries, among other places.

I smiled broadly as I recalled their faces or deeds. "How lucky I am," I remember thinking, "to have had so many good people in my life."

(I also admit to sometimes feeling deep sadness that some people from whom I expected more had not much involved themselves in my struggles.)

Next, I tried to remember where I was in the coming out process when these wonderful heterosexuals touched me. The needier I was, the more significant to me was their outreach.

And then I thanked God for their loving, healing, encouraging, and inspiring presence in my life.

Mary Grix was an early entry on my list. She was the very proper mother of my best friend, Henry. The only daughter of a prominent Detroit family, she was decidedly old-fashioned in her appearance, wearing, as I recall, mostly black straight-line dresses and little makeup, with her gray hair pulled back into a neat bun.

By her demeanor, you might have guessed that she would be the last person who'd embrace an openly gay man in the early 1970s, but when I came out to her on the eve of my public announcement, she said simply, "As long as you are happy, dear. That is what is important."

Twenty-some years later, I can say that to myself, and have had far more dramatic displays of support from others, but Henry's mother's reassuring words and manner back then left an indelible impression. I knew that no matter how bad it got, Mrs. Grix loved me.

I knew my friend Mildred McIver loved me too. She was a black female typesetter at *The Michigan Catholic* during my labor dispute with them. We were self-described "good buddies" who laughed, sang, and carried on together in a special way that compensated for the isolation we each felt.

During a week in which most people at work were not talking to me because they were angry about the attention my coming out had brought to the newspaper, Mildred called me to the back room. In tears of frustration she confided that she was being "asked" to sign a petition intended to distance the employees from me in the public's eye.

"If I don't sign, I'll pay for it," she said. "But if I do sign, I'll hate myself."

"Sign it," I insisted, noting forever that she was the only one of the employees who shared with me her discomfort in putting her name on the petition.

A few weeks later, the paper fired me, and I never saw Mildred again. Yet, after these many years, her name is now on my list because her loving outreach at a very traumatic time reminded me that I was not alone.

So too is Gracie's. Gracie was my eighty-year-old inner-city landlady when I was on my hunger strike. Though she never spoke directly to me about homosexuality, she would sneak into my apartment each morning and leave on my table a vase of garden-cut flowers and any newspaper article about my fast. "How ya doin' today?" she would ask. "Anything you need?"

I never asked Mary, Mildred, or Gracie why they were so kind, or how they became comfortable enough with the issue to extend themselves so readily to me.

When Dr. Gregory Herek did his groundbreaking research on the roots of homophobia,[3] he concluded that there were three basic causes for anti-gay bias. He designated them "Experiential Attitudes," "Defensive Attitudes," and "Symbolic Attitudes."

Briefly, in the first instance, the individual has had a bad experience, perhaps as a child, with a same-sex person. He or she knows or assumes that the perpetrator was homosexual, and concludes that all gay men and women are bad people. Thus, the individual's horrible experience creates intolerant attitudes.

Individuals whose attitudes fall into the second category feel personally threatened by homosexuality and by gay people because they are uncomfortable with their own sexuality and possibly insecure in their gender identity. Their defensiveness makes it difficult for them to learn positive information about the issue.

Individuals whose attitudes fall into the third category are hostile for no personal reasons but because they feel homosexuality diminishes values that they hold sacred. One such value could be the loyalty they have to a church group, organization, or circle of friends that is homophobic.

I suspect that the positive, pro-gay attitudes of people such as Mary, Mildred, and Gracie are influenced in parallel ways.

For instance, many supportive heterosexuals have had wonderful experiences with gay, lesbian, and bisexual people and can't tolerate the thought of their family members or friends being mistreated by others.

My aunt Joan is a perfect example. She doesn't understand all the ins and outs of sexual orientation, nor why the Church takes the position it does, but she has powerful feelings of affection for her two gay nephews, and nothing will interfere with that. She doesn't comprehend why others don't feel as she does, and is pained to hear examples of the bigotry we encounter.

Other straight men and women may not know any gay people but feel very secure in themselves and very clear how unreasonable and personally limiting anti-gay bias is. I have met these individuals on college campuses and in my corporate trainings. One of the most refreshing encounters was with three heterosexual college football players who shared an apartment.

"Homophobia sucks," one said succinctly after my talk.

"People think we're gay because we all get on the same bed and watch TV," privately explained his roommate.

"On the bed or *in* the bed?" I asked incredulously.

"We're all under the covers at the same time. So what?" he appropriately challenged.

"We're friends," piped in the third man. "We don't want to give up what we've got because some people are uptight about guys being close. It's their problem."

And then there are those for whom homophobia and heterosexism are completely incompatible with their values of charity and justice. To stay silent in the face of such bigotry would undermine their personal commitment to spiritual health.

Coretta Scott King comes to mind. So too does my friend Johnnetta Cole, former president of the historically black Spelman College in Atlanta.

"Ours is a new friendship," she wrote, "but it is grounded in values that are both ancient and priceless. We, you and I, have sincere respect and appreciation for the ways in which we are different from each other. We truly believe in education and insist that whether the instruction is going on in a Spelman classroom or in one of Brian's workshops, the world will be better off because of it."

Undoubtedly, what motivates most heterosexual people to invest themselves in gay liberation results from a myriad of reasons that impact not only why, but also how, when, and how much they involve themselves in the struggle.

My good friend Carol Dopp, whose picture is among those on the "table of honor" in my office, believes that heterosexual supporters like herself go through stages of "coming out" similar to those experienced by gay women and men. If and how one moves through those stages is heavily influenced by factors such as one's religious, cultural, and educational background, personal experiences, social skills, and cherished values. I think she's right.

In the beginning of the process, potential heterosexual Allies recognize the inappropriateness of hostile behaviors toward homosexuals, but are unsure of what to do and how to do it. They also worry about how involvement in the issue will impact their image.

It's understandable that, during the early stages of their development, potential Allies will often weigh how speaking out against anti-gay bias will affect their important relationships with family members, friends, colleagues, and their faith community. If the risk of loss seems too high, they will probably step back. If not, they will continue to explore the issue by safely seeking out more information, which may involve buying a book, watching a TV documentary, or attending an educational program.

If touched more personally, perhaps by attending a powerful workshop on gay issues or having a close friend or family member come out, heterosexual Allies generally enter the next stage of involvement. As their concern deepens, straight men and women often seek out individuals with similar values who can support their new behaviors. They will listen for gay-positive comments from their peers. They may communicate their thoughts to someone they know to be gay. And, as Carol did, they might join a group such as GLSTN or P-FLAG (see Resources, "Support").

In time, heterosexual supporters may come to identify personally with the oppression gay people face. Their level of awareness of heterosexism and homophobia becomes keen, the reasons for their commitment are clear, and their patience with insensitive friends and inappropriate behavior is very limited.

In my office there are pictures of a number of heterosexual people who have made this journey. They are my Friends, my Allies, my Advocates, and my Heroes. On one particular tilt-top table, there are a handful of photographs of people with whom I feel particularly close and for whom I am especially grateful. Their smiles from across the room continually remind me that I have straight friends who are with me in battle and want me to trust that they understand.

Mary Lee Tatum's twinkling eyes communicate such a message. She was my best friend as well as my business partner in corporate training. She also has the distinction of being the first heterosexual I ever truly trusted.

"ML," as she was affectionately called, was best known as a high school sexuality educator in Falls Church, Virginia, who was tireless in her advocacy for sexual self-esteem. As such, her life involved counseling gay students, the spouses of gay people, and any homosexual, bisexual, transsexual, or transvestite lucky enough to wander into her embracing arms.

Mary Lee's awareness of and commitment to gay civil rights sprang from her personal experiences and from her faith. As a student at Washington State University, she met and married a closeted gay man. He became a Presbyterian minister, she got her master's in health education, and they raised two wonderful daughters. Then Bill came out, he and ML separated, he contracted AIDS, and she and the girls nursed him until his death.

An old-time, unabashed liberal whose children's early memories are of anti-war demonstrations on the Great Mall in Washington, D.C., Mary Lee believed in a New Testament gospel of justice and took her lead for action from the Sermon on the Mount. Her adult education classes at the Presbyterian church focused on the impact of racism, sexism, heterosexism, and all the other "evils" she saw as contrary to those values.

I met Mary Lee at the Annual Workshop on Sexuality at Thornfield,[4] in Cazenovia, New York. I'd just finished telling my coming out story to the group when she asked if we could talk privately.

She told me that she loved, and had her high school students read, my open letter to Anita Bryant.[5] She also opened herself up, describing her difficult life with Bill.

Then, as she reached out and took my hand, Mary Lee said, "Your talk was so moving, Brian, but I know there's a lot more pain than you let on. It really hurts, doesn't it?"

I looked at her in disbelief. No heterosexual had ever asked me this question before. Immediately I teared up. Somehow I trusted that she understood. Her eyes, the gentle touch and warmth of her hand, and the sympathizing expression of her lips told me so.

At that instant, she was my mother, my sisters, the nuns who taught me in school, the Church, and all of the female figures in my life from whom at the time I hungered in vain to receive true understanding and unconditional love. And for the many years afterward during which we were inseparable friends, I never had reason to doubt for an instant her sensitivity or commitment to the issue or to me.

I loved Mary Lee as I had loved no other friend. And when we talked on the phone, as we did three or four nights of the week, or when we sat together drinking white wine in a hotel bar after a tough day of training, I knew that I was completely loved by her. Nowhere to be found was that all-too-familiar gnawing voice from within: "She'd like you better, she'd be more relaxed, she'd really prefer it, if you were straight."

When she died in an automobile accident in a 1991 rainstorm, I lost a best friend and soul mate, and the gay, lesbian, and bisexual community lost a true Hero.

Mary Lee was publicly scourged at home and throughout the country by conservative women's groups and others who hated her for her efforts at sexuality education and her well-known support of gay issues. Yet despite their relentless personal attacks, she never backed off.

Carol picked me up at the airport for Mary Lee's funeral. We stopped for flowers and placed them at the tree where she died. Students from the school milled around us, crying, holding each other, and placing notes and their own bouquets at the base of the sorry oak.

Carol was Mary Lee's young protégé, and with excitement and pride she immediately took over her adult education class and the job of hosting the transsexual men and women's meetings at the church. Now head of counseling in a prestigious Washington, D.C., high school, she is also a sexuality educator with a long list of grateful gay, lesbian, and bisexual clients and friends.

Carol speaks to her students about homosexuality from a personal perspective. She knows and loves gay people, she explains, and is committed to the cause of civil rights.

"But my job with you is to provide accurate information about sexuality so that you all can draw your own conclusions," she assures them. "I'm not here to tell you what to think."

Beyond having a lesbian roommate by chance in college, Carol did not have much exposure to the subject. She has no gay relatives of whom she is aware. Yet, once she was exposed to the issue, getting involved seemed like the only thing to do. She was encouraged in her efforts by her friendship with me, her faith, and her admiration for her mentor, ML.

"It also doesn't hurt to have a husband who's supportive," adds Carol. And Pam would agree.

Pam Wilson, one of my best friends and my current business partner, has promised me she'll never marry a man who is homophobic.

Pam hates the picture of her that I display in my office, but is proud of the rainbow frame in which it sits. She purchased it as a birthday gift from an AIDS support organization.

As a black woman, Pam knows the sting and power of bigotry; that is one reason why she's so uncompromising in her commitment to gay civil rights. But it has been a learning experience.

"When I first started out, I was very heterosexist," she explained to the corporate audience during our training. "Like many of you, I had no exposure to the issue. In fact, as a child I remember my aunt pointing out a person on the street and saying, 'There goes one of those he-shes.' That's what I thought all gay people looked like."

Today, Pam's "gaydar" is as fine-tuned as mine.

"I met a gay couple on the cruise," she told me upon her return from a vacation recently.

"I had noticed this man who was very thin, pale, and had some KS [Kaposi's sarcoma] lesions," she explained. "He would walk up and down the deck by himself. So I gave him a big smile and said, 'How ya doin'?' He stopped, smiled back, and started talking. When I told him about my work, he began to open up."

Besides cofacilitating my workshops, Pam is a sexuality educator and diversity trainer who works with groups throughout the country. When she encounters individuals whom she thinks might be gay, lesbian, or bisexual she casually but consciously brings up her efforts to fight homophobia in the hope they will trust her and come out. They usually do.

"The guy confided to me that he and his lover were on the cruise alone," Pam said, "so I spent time with them and encouraged them to join our group, if they wanted to."

Advocates such as Carol and Pam keep their eyes and ears open for opportunities to be supportive. For them it can mean speaking up at a family reunion, in a teacher's lounge, or on an airplane when someone crosses the line. It also has meant donning a pink triangle T-shirt and walking in a Gay Pride parade.

None of this is done without effort or consequence. It's often very challenging to be an Advocate. Carol's insistence on respectful language for gay people in her classroom, for instance, has been interpreted by some angry parents as an endorsement of homosexuality. Pam's invitation to the gay man with AIDS to join her friends on the cruise has required that she educate her friends or find new ones who are comfortable with her outreach to others.

"Sometimes the room goes real quiet when I call a family member on a homophobic comment," explains Carol.

"After the parade, an attendant at the parking lot took a look at my T-shirt and moaned, 'Are you one of *them?* What a waste!' " reported Pam.

But the hassles they get from others don't stop my straight friends from speaking up, and that's why I trust them.

Alison Deming is another trusted friend who doesn't back off on her support of gay issues. But her picture appears among the others less for her numerous daily efforts on behalf of gay, lesbian, and bisexual people and more for the important role she plays in Ray's and my life.

A constantly evolving and inquisitive family therapist and sexuality educator, she is a treasured member of our family, acting, in part, as the hip mother figure we always wanted to be able to take to gay movies and introduce to gay friends. She's the "Mom" with no gay children of her own who travels to Washington, D.C., to view the AIDS quilt and who weeps as she walks among the panels. She's the Mom who travels hours to hear me speak, and who, no matter how many times she has heard my story, assures me, "You were wonderful!"

Our own Auntie Mame and Anna Madrigal rolled into one, she has many times held court at our Thanksgiving dinner table and was one of only a handful of heterosexual friends present at our tenth anniversary celebration.

Again, having no family ties to the issue of homosexuality, Alison came to her awareness of gay oppression by her own struggles as a woman, by her faith, by the education she received about human sexuality, and by her friendship with people like us.

Now a volunteer for the Peace Corps in the Caribbean, this sixty-five-year-old daughter of a Presbyterian minister raised a family of three boys and a girl and then went back to school to get a degree in counseling. In addition to the many gay clients she was forced to leave for her new assignment, she also regretfully had to resign from the board of the local AIDS task force.

In my office, as I look at Alison's playful pose, I wish my table had far more space for pictures of the many, many people on my growing list of Friends, Allies, Advocates, and Heroes. So too do I wish I had more room here to tell their stories. It troubles me that I don't, and I apologize to those who are reading this wondering why their friendship and hard work aren't being acknowledged.

You know who you are. Please trust that I know who you are, too. Thank you for everything you do.

Of course, this does make me wonder if and how I appear on any lists my heterosexual friends have made for themselves. To what extent do these good people see me as an advocate battling *their* oppression, whether it be racism, sexism, ageism, anti-Semitism, or any other bigotry? Though I feel as if I've worked hard to confront my own biases and those of others, I might be painfully disappointed to learn that they don't see in my actions the concern I have about their well-being.

It would break my heart to think that my friends felt that I didn't care sufficiently about the injustices they face. As they do with me, I want them to trust that they're loved and not alone. They're my family. An attack on one of them because of his or her skin color, gender, age, faith, physical appearance, or ability is an attack on me.

Beyond my love for them, I fight their battles because it's the right and just thing to do. If I, as a gay person, want to live in a world free of oppression and want others to be advocates in my battle, I must be willing to do the same for them. As my dear friend Sol Gordon so aptly reminds us, "If we don't hang together, we hang separately."

When I tell audiences the story of Bob Stark, the track coach, stepping forward to ensure that my name remained on the high school award plaque, I recall a statement attributed to eighteenth-century British statesman Edmund Burke: "The only thing necessary for the triumph of evil is for good people to do nothing."

9

ABOUT
RELIGION AND SPIRITUALITY

As I remember my meeting with the bishop these many years later, I was nervous, though self-assured, and I felt he was quite uncomfortable. I was the young gay writer whose popular column had just been dropped by the weekly Catholic newspaper. He was the liberal, forty-four-year-old auxiliary bishop of the diocese, helping to hold the fort while the cardinal was in Rome.

It was 1974, a time of major upheaval in society and in my church. I had asked to meet with Bishop Thomas Gumbleton in the hope he would be my advocate both in my employment dispute with the newspaper and in my efforts to help the church better understand and address the painful dilemma of the gay Catholic.

I remember being very disappointed by what I experienced as his cool though polite reserve. I was naive, romantic, and idealistic. I had fantasized that his response, consistent with his reputation as a social justice advocate, would be a heroic embrace, like that of Pope Innocent III to the passionate young Francis of Assisi. But he was cautious, as I now understand he was bound to be, seeing me not as another Francis but rather as a loose cannon.

My disappointment with the bishop has to be understood in context. I had a passionate love for and dependence on the Catholic Church. It was more important to me than my own family.

Having been born in a Catholic hospital; schooled by nuns, brothers, and priests through sixteen years of Catholic education; and indoctrinated with a lifetime of Mass and the sacraments, I saw myself as a child of the church and the bishop as my father.

Since childhood I had secretly aspired to be a saint. I was an altar boy and played priest as a child at home. The eighth-grade nun proclaimed I was a "prince of a boy." In high school I was chosen for the Christian Leadership Award. In college I was mockingly referred to as "the dorm Catholic." I studied to be a religious brother (albeit for only six weeks), and taught religion to high school students after work at the Catholic newspaper. With the exception of my homosexuality, which I did not see as a sin, I was in the minds of many people the *ideal* Catholic.

Because of the bishop's reputation for advocating on behalf of the oppressed, I was sure we shared the same understanding of Christ's message—love and do good. Recalling my unrealistic expectations of the church and the young bishop's cautious response to me helps one to understand the very painful sense of abandonment that many gay people of nearly all faiths have had with their religious institutions.

For me, and for many gay, lesbian, and bisexual people I know, expecting but not receiving a loving, comforting embrace from the people we had followed and admired for their spirituality led us to a bitterness and cynicism about religion and the people who preach it. Sometimes, it also prompted an angry rejection of the basics of the faith and even a hostile questioning of the existence of God.

Having experienced ourselves on the floor rather than on the lap of our religious institutions, many of us began to look elsewhere for comfort and a sense of belonging. Perhaps we would find it in a different denomination. Perhaps we would find it on our own.

Those of us who stayed within our faiths often found ourselves in a wrestling match with other, far more conservative people for the sacred artifacts of our beliefs, such as the Bible or Talmud, and for some, the cross and Jesus as we knew him. Increasingly, we were outflanked and intimidated by the screams of those who quoted religious texts judgmentally and wore T-shirts that proclaimed: "Turn or Burn."

Anita Bryant, champion of the anti-gay "Save Our Children" movement in Florida in the late 1970s, was pictured as a praying mother fighting against godless, militant, predatory homosexuals. "Wait!" many of us protested in self-defense. "We pray too. We're not godless." But few people seemed either to hear us or to believe us.

Religious fundamentalists and conservative politicians declared a public war against homosexuals. Many of us looked desperately to our powerful mainline denominations to speak out in our behalf against such frightening, hateful rhetoric, as we had seen them do in the civil rights movement.

Instead, what we felt we heard was their approving silence and what we felt we saw was all of our religious leaders, including black pastors with whom we had marched for civil rights, dining together with our enemies at ecumenical breakfast meetings on the united theme of "Save the Family."

Many of us felt betrayed, abandoned, and terribly isolated. It was an experience not unlike the day Ray and I and two gay friends went to the Six Flags Over Georgia amusement park to celebrate a birthday and unexpectedly found ourselves among forty thousand Born Again Christians. It was terrifying to be surrounded by people who seemed to hate us simply because we were gay.

Nearly every encounter between gay people and the spokespersons for most mainline religions was experienced by both sides as a battle for survival. Nearly every confrontation was framed as a tug-of-war for the cherished, life-giving sources of our faith. Eventually though, feeling completely unsupported, many gay, lesbian, and bisexual people let go of the rope.

GOD HATES FAGS declared the signs carried along the route of the St. Patrick's Day parade, outside the memorial service for the man who died of AIDS, and on the corner across the street from the displayed quilt. And "Fags hate God," angrily mumbled more than one walking-wounded gay Christian person for whom the formerly inspiring cross had been twisted by the masses into a frightening swastika and for whom the formerly comforting Bible had been condensed into poisonous bile. For me, even the sweet name of Jesus, now slapped on car bumpers next to Confederate flags, invoked incessantly in livid anti-gay diatribes, and borrowed freely for slogans such as "Kill a Queer for Christ" was drained eventually of its reputation for love. My former best friend, it seemed, now hung out with those who bullied me.

Such disenfranchisement was not the intention of the young bishop who sat so nervously with me as I asked him for his support. It was not his wish that I leave the church nor the wish of any of the religious men and women I had so admired but who so disappointed me. They were and are good people. But with regard to homosexuality, they felt ill-prepared to respond in any manner other than with awkward, arms-length fear. Thus, the expectations of most gay Christians and Jews were unrealistic at that time in our history.

My meeting with Bishop Gumbleton twenty-some years ago offers the opportunity to look at why and how reasonable people in the various religious denominations have so often failed, in my opinion, to respond to the gay issue with the courage, fortitude, and love that have characterized many of their other responses to issues of faith and morals. The story of my journey and that of the bishop can also help one understand how people can change, and why, I believe, there is hope for us all.

Young, intensely religious people, as I was in 1974, generally take quite literally the messages of their faith they have had repeatedly reinforced in sermons, in spiritual songs, in inspiring stories, and in religious films. "God is love," I learned, and "they who abide in love abide in God and God in them," and "I was hungry and you gave me something to eat. I was naked and you gave me something to wear."

When I sat across from the bishop, I envisioned myself as the robbed and beaten man by the side of the road and I anticipated he would be my Samaritan, tending to me regardless of the consequences. I romantically saw myself as the leper who, though frightening, would be embraced by the true believer. I also hoped that I was living as Jesus instructed, suffering persecution for justice's sake. I was being publicly scourged with death threats, obscene phone calls, and hateful letters for acknowledging that I was gay. Surely, I thought, the church would comfort, defend, and protect me. The church was my life and certainly my future.

What I did not take into consideration at the time was how ill-prepared the bishop was for my visit, both as a spokesperson for the church's sexual theology and as a man.

The Catholic Church had seemingly clear guidelines for appropriate sexual expression. For sex to be licit it must be between a man and a woman who are married to each other and who have as their goals a willingness to create new life and the affirmation of their loving, faithful union. Furthermore, for the activity to be licit, the sex must involve penile-vaginal intercourse. Any activity outside of these guidelines would be considered against God's will and therefore immoral and sinful.

Artificial means of birth control, masturbation, fellatio, cunnilingus, sex before or outside of marriage, and homosexuality would in and of themselves be immoral activities. That is what the bishop was charged to believe and to teach. That is what every Catholic is charged to believe. How could I as a Catholic propose to violate those rules and how could I expect the bishop to support me?

Quite simply, the reason I felt comfortable presenting myself as gay and Catholic is that I had seen others speak of themselves as birth controllers and Catholic, masturbators and Catholic, non-coitus-oriented and Catholic, divorced and Catholic. Further, I had watched and listened as various Catholic leaders had come to their defense.

In college, for instance, a priest told me to quit coming to confession to report masturbation as a sin. It was *not* a sin, he said, and there was nothing to forgive. Other priests privately counseled Catholic couples to follow their conscience on birth control. The priest editor of my newspaper was rumored to be among those performing marriages for divorced Catholics. Why not, then, expect such support for homosexuality? Logically, I could. But the issues were quite different at the gut level. The bishop wasn't raised since childhood to fear and hate those who practiced birth control.

What Bishop Gumbleton brought to our meeting beyond Catholic doctrine was a lifetime of unchallenged myths and unflattering images of people like me. "Faggot," "sissy," "pansy," "homo," and "queer" were among the names he'd heard. "Promiscuous," "child molester," "sexual deviant," "unnatural," "chosen lifestyle," "gender confusion," and "predator" were among the frightening myths with which he had been raised. So too had the nuns, priests, brothers, and lay Catholics from whom I had hoped to receive understanding and support. I unrealistically assumed that their faith-inspired commitment to social justice would enable them to overcome the culturally based biases that incapacitated others.

A few weeks after the meeting with the bishop, I did the only thing I could think of to get the attention of the church I so loved. Frustrated by the seeming lack of serious response by the religious leaders of my church to the alienation, isolation, and extraordinary fear of gay people, and besieged by a hateful, threatening public response, I began what I anticipated could be a fast until death. I said that I wouldn't eat any food or drink any liquid other than water until the local Catholic bishops pledged they would commit themselves to educating the clergy about homosexuality. Education, I believed, was the most important weapon we had against this intolerance, apathy, and fear.

I had learned of the hunger strike, popularized by black social activist Dick Gregory, when I interviewed a priest who had fasted over American involvement in the Vietnam War. I appreciated it as a nonviolent, biblically sound way to call attention to an important issue. My hope was to convince the justice-oriented people in my church that injustice against gay people was as serious as injustice against blacks (for whom so many of us had marched), Latinos (for whom so many of us had participated in organized boycotts), and Vietnamese (for whom we had risked arrest to end the bombings).

For much of my fast, I prayed in the small chapel we had created in my home. The regimen was simple. A daily Epsom salts bath and an enema to clean the body of food-related poisons, and at least a gallon of water consumed a day.

While I was on the fast, many gay Catholics from across the country wrote and called to encourage me on. Dignity, the national organization of gay Catholics, sponsored a day of fasting in support. Considerable media attention was given to the fast. Both local and national newspapers carried updates, as well as pro and con editorials and letters to the editor. One syndicated conservative Catholic columnist declared me a "heretic."

A letter, signed by Bishops Thomas Gumbleton and Joseph Imesch, was delivered to me seventeen days into the fast. They said, in part, ". . . we are aware of the pain, suffering, and discrimination that is at times inflicted upon the homosexual. While the Catholic Church, in view of its moral teaching, cannot endorse or condone overt homosexual acts, we have a serious obligation to root out structures and attitudes that discriminate against the homosexual as a person. We will exert our leadership in behalf of this effort. We hope for your continued cooperation with us in trying to achieve this goal."

With great relief and excitement, I ended the fast. I had been heard, I felt. Some theologians were making public statements about the issue. The Episcopal bishop of Michigan wrote to the cardinal archbishop of Detroit on my behalf. "The church will now confront discrimination against gay people," I thought.

The evening I ended my fast, however, I received a call at home from the business manager of the Catholic newspaper where I worked. I was fired. A subsequent out-of-court settlement that was made with the archdiocese forbade me to ever again seek employment in the Church. Later, I was told that Bishops Gumbleton and Imesch had signed their letter to me under pressure. Monsignor Clement Kern, a highly respected champion of the oppressed in Detroit, had allegedly camped outside of the bishops' offices until they signed the document that would end my fast.

Discouraged but not defeated, I continued to work at changing my church's attitudes about gay people. In 1976 I wrote an article, "The Sad Dilemma of the Gay Catholic," for *The U.S. Catholic,* a widely read and highly respected national magazine. To my great surprise and delight, my article won the Catholic Press Association's highest honor, Best Magazine Article of the Year. But I didn't win the embrace of the spiritual leaders whose support I sought by writing the piece.

Also that year, I represented gay Catholic concerns at the historic U.S. bishops' bicentennial hearing, "A Call to Action," in Detroit, and I secured, to my own amazement, a majority of the lay and religious delegates' endorsements of gay-positive amendments. Gay Catholics throughout the country were elated and very hopeful, but the American bishops later rejected all of the resolutions and, in so doing, left us feeling rejected too.

Mistakenly, I had felt that if I was cogent enough with my words, written or spoken, I could create the understanding I sought. I felt that if I was spiritual enough, suffered enough, was loyal enough, patient enough, respected enough, they would change, and their seemingly icy, political response would melt into a courageous battle on our behalf. But it didn't happen.

I began to accept that they—meaning the shepherds of the church—really didn't care about me. Dignity chapters were forced out of Catholic facilities, the Vatican referred to my sexual orientation as "seriously disordered," and we were told that those gay people who were being beaten and murdered had to take responsibility for bringing it upon themselves.

My hope that American bishops would stand up to such nonsense was diminished. Rather than be my allies, those in the hierarchy became my adversaries. They did so as much with their silence as with their deeds. When I and other gay people would testify before state representatives on behalf of legislation that would protect homosexuals from being fired from their jobs or evicted from their apartments solely because of their sexual orientation, a representative of the local bishop would generally be in the audience awaiting his or her turn to testify against the legislation.

Feeling hurt and betrayed, I got angry. When I finally accepted that I was unwanted by my institution, like so many other gay Christians and Jews I knew, I sought retribution. I became preoccupied with the weaknesses of my church and angrily celebrated its seeming defeats.

I took pleasure, for instance, in reading of parishes closing because of the lack of priests. I took smug satisfaction in hearing of priests being arrested in male porn theaters and rest stops and of others being charged with molesting children. I took particular delight in the public humiliation of television evangelists who got caught with prostitutes or defrauding their flock.

My hatred of the institutional church was like an ulcer. It began eating at my insides. I wanted retribution for being disowned. I responded to what I perceived as hate with hate. The well was poisoned.

My spirituality, sadly, was now *reactive* rather than *proactive*. Instead of freely exploring my relationship to God and how it was impacted by my being gay, I was tossed emotionally back and forth by the church-related events around me. Instead of smelling the roses and celebrating my life, I was preoccupied with what I perceived to be the stench of the church and I begrudged them their happiness. If I couldn't control the church's response to me, I wanted to control the world's response to the church.

This became crystal clear to me one day while shopping at a discount appliance store in Massachusetts. While strolling through the television department, I noticed that every unit was displaying the face of the cardinal archbishop of Boston, one of the most conservative prelates in the country, a man who as an auxiliary bishop had seemingly risen to speak against every "Call to Action" amendment I proposed.

He represented to me all that I hated about the Catholic hierarchy. I found him calculating, grandstanding, phony in his public piety, and horribly homophobic. He was my enemy, and so I eliminated him. On television after television, perhaps sixty or seventy sets in all, I pushed the channel button in search of a less threatening face. Any face would do. Not only will I not have to look at him, I thought, but he will lose his audience.

Years later, when I reported my deed in a speech to the delegates at Dignity's national convention, the gay Catholic men and women laughed and cheered with delight.

"But you don't understand," I explained as the applause subsided. "Instead of wasting the time it took me to turn off all of those televisions, I could have been doing something positive for myself, something proactive, not reactive. I could have been *shopping!*"

"So, are you still a Catholic?" someone asked.

"No," I said with an uncertain degree of confidence and conviction, "I am not."

I remember returning home from that Dignity convention very frustrated that I had not done a good job in communicating to the audience the logical steps of my journey from being the loyal Catholic son of the church to a position of pantheist whose mantra was Meher Baba's ever-popular teaching, "Do your best and leave the rest to God. Don't worry. Be happy." I could clearly identify for them the various road signs that had marked my journey within the church. What felt terribly awkward was identifying the road signs that I had followed out of the Church.

Multiple factors, I suppose, led me out of the church and into my current spiritual journey. Some had to do with the church and some had to do with me. I was, of course, crushed by my unrealized expectations of the Catholic Church. Like the child who feels neglected and abused, I eventually came to feel unwelcome and unsafe in my own home. Also, as I continued growing in self-esteem as a gay man, I became less and less reliant on the approval of heterosexuals and more and more intolerant of anyone or anything that did not fully support me as a gay man.

While I imagine I will forever be a cultural Catholic, happily reminiscing with other people raised Catholic about the fun, idiosyncratic aspects of our childhood, I no longer experience myself as a member of the family. I lost patience with the process of educating my church family about homosexuality and lost confidence in the ability of the American hierarchy to challenge Vatican pronouncements on gay issues.

I was a pre–Vatican II child whose faith came of age under the exciting, daring, courageous leadership of Pope John XXIII. Most everything institutional since his death has felt uninspired and reactionary. The Catholic Church appeared to me to be more like a big business than a community of believers whose members were known by their love for each other. The emphasis seemed to be on the letter of the law rather than on the experience of the human being.

So, one sign that I might point to as leading me out of the church read, "Brian, we don't like you as you are." And the sign that I planted read, "Church, I don't like you as you are either."

Another sign that led me into the desert indicated that my theology and that of the institutional Church were heading in different directions. When I tried to take Jesus literally and accept his invitation, "Do as I have done," I eventually questioned my belief that he was the *sole* son of God.

I began to wonder if Jesus wasn't inviting me to experience my own humanity and my own divinity to the same degree he had. Instead of my God, then, he became more my older and wiser brother. I subsequently began questioning everything I had previously believed to be true, such as the virgin birth of Jesus to Mary; the trinity of Father, Son, and Holy Spirit; God the "Father" (as opposed to God the *Mother* or the genderless parent); eternal punishment in hell; the criteria for sainthood; the infallibility of the pope; and other issues.

I began to wonder about the fate of those who didn't embrace Jesus as the sole son of God, and of those who had never heard of him. One popular televangelist said that God doesn't hear the prayers of Jews. I knew that wasn't true of the God whom I sought in prayer. All religions, in my mind, eventually gained equal footing as honest attempts to understand and be in union with God, a "hero with a thousand faces,"[1] to use Joseph Campbell's phrase.

I decided to start from scratch and examine my basic beliefs. After many years of reflection I concluded that I trusted there is a power greater than myself, whom I refer to as "Higher Power" or "God." How it works in my everyday life is a mystery to me. I also believe that Jesus, among others, had amazing experiences with God from which I can learn a great deal. Likewise, I believe that others can profit from *my* experience of God, as they can from their own.

So, not only do I not consider myself a Catholic. I came to understand that I was probably no longer a Christian.

"Of course you're a Christian," insisted my younger sister, Maureen, who, at the time, identified herself as Born Again. "You're the nicest person I know!"

"Being nice doesn't mean that you're a Christian," I said, "and being Christian doesn't mean that you're nice. Christians believe that Jesus is God, that he died for our sins, and that he rose from the dead. I'm not sure I believe all of that." I figure there are a lot of nice people who don't believe all of that, and that the God with whom I seek to be in harmony is more invested in how I *behave* than in what I *believe.*

"But are you religious?" I am asked.

"No, I am *spiritual,*" I will say.

Years ago, a Jesuit priest by the name of Ed Farrell wrote the book *Prayer Is a Hunger.*[2] I love the imagery because I experience myself as having a hunger to know and be in union with my God. I experience myself as constantly in prayer. Like Siddhartha in Herman Hesse's tale,[3] I am on a journey to find out the truth about life. When confronted with the truth embodied by the Buddha, Siddhartha decided not to follow him but to travel on his own because he felt he couldn't learn the truth from a teacher but instead had to experience it for himself.

A conservative Presbyterian theologian once told me during a radio debate, "An active homosexual who looks to the Bible for salvation is looking down the barrel of a shotgun." When the Buddha I encounter provides a "truth" that is inconsistent with my experience, I reject the Buddha and I embrace the experience. I reject any teacher or any belief that doesn't affirm my sexual orientation or accept the basic goodness of my physically expressed love. My experience of making love to another man tells me that those who say "God hates fags" are wrong. That belief or any sanitized version of it has no relevance in my life. It doesn't nurture my soul, it abuses it.

I hunger for ways to understand God that help me affirm who I am. I was starving in the Church and so I wandered into the desert. Like the Jews freed from Egypt, I left the comfort and conveniences of my home in slavery to search as a free gay man for my own promised land of milk and honey.

Sometimes in my desire to be fed, I have wandered back into Catholic churches, not unlike the child of the dysfunctional home who keeps returning in the hope of finding something different. The smell of incense, the sight of candles flickering, and the peaceful silence found within can rekindle for me happy fantasies of feeling safe. I may miss the seeming certainty of those innocent years, but I know that I can't stay seated in that church. To do so would be to invite back those horribly uncomfortable and debilitating feelings of anger, hurt, and frustration. And so I depart. But before doing so, I usually leave a little reminder that I was there, a little claim to the space that once was my home. I either light a candle or place in the petitions box a request for prayers "that the church might fully embrace gay people and those with AIDS."

On my journey in the desert I also wander into bookstores in search of signs that I am heading in the right direction. There I have found helpful maps like *The Power of Myth*,[4] *Becoming a Man*,[5] *Christianity, Social Tolerance and Homosexuality*,[6] *The Celestine Prophecy*,[7] *Gay Soul*,[8] *Mutant Message Down Under*,[9] *The Way of the Peaceful Warrior*[10] and *Many Lives, Many Masters*.[11] In these and others works I have found encouragement for my belief that the essence of spirituality is found not in judgment but in affirmation of self and of others who are on the journey home. Similarly encouraging signs have been found in music, in plays, and in films of the same philosophy, creating powerful moments of inspiration not unlike those I felt as a youngster in traditionally religious materials.

My hunger has also led me into the incredibly exciting professional field of human sexuality. There I have found a bold reclaiming and celebration of that which is human, and therefore divine. In an amazing community that is gay, straight, and bisexual; male, female, and transgender; I experience the same loving openness and commitment to the ideals of equality that I remember feeling during the early days of Church renewal.

Sexuality educators who stretch beyond their levels of cultural comfort to understand and address the painful journey of a transsexual, a transvestite, or some other social "outcast" remind me of the pride I felt for those clergy, religious, and lay Catholics who marched in Selma for integration and in Washington, D.C., against the war in Vietnam. Among sexuality educators I experience a family that is committed to the incarnation of body and spirit, to a gospel of social justice, and to relieving the human suffering that is caused by ignorance and fear. The compassion, courage, and commitment of most sexuality educators I find to be *holy*. The healing moments many of us have had with social outcasts I find to be truly *sacred*.

Regrettably, the causes that this new family of faith takes on with such passion often pit us against the family of my youth, the institutional church.

My hunger for harmony with God thankfully also brought me into contact with the twelve-step programs of recovery[12] and into the remarkably inspiring community of men and women who take those steps. With them, I am learning to accept that I am unable to control my life or the lives of others, and learning to turn my life over to God. When I was able to acknowledge my codependency and to acknowledge my unhealthy reliance upon white wine for comfort, I was able to begin to reconnect with a God I had abandoned to those who I felt had condemned me with their ugly words or with their silence.

I welcomed the name Higher Power for my God, for it allowed me to avoid my terribly conflicted past efforts to name and define God. When I was able to say with confidence, "God, grant me the serenity to accept the things I cannot change, the courage to change the things I can, and the wisdom to know the difference," I began to let go of my anger and resentment at those in the Church, including Jesus, who had hurt or disappointed me.

Much of my life has been filled with resentments. "Why *me?*" I wondered. "How could the newspaper drop my column?" "How could the diocese fire me?" "How could people I so admired be so conspicuously silent on the pain of gay people, on the outrageous behavior of individual bishops and the Vatican, and on the plight of those persons with AIDS?" "How could Jesus allow his name so to be taken in vain?" "How could God allow hateful anti-gay behavior by so-called Christians not only to go unpunished but seemingly to be rewarded?"

My efforts at recovery have prompted me to begin to understand the spiritual and physical unhealthiness of the "victim mentality" and to begin letting go of my mountain of resentments. In my hunger for spiritual healthiness I'm also learning to try to better understand the journeys made by others, and to realize that I can't control the behavior or reactions of other people. What I can control are my expectations of and reactions to them.

I've come to believe that every person is on an individual spiritual journey. How each of us responds to the opportunities life provides us to love and to grow is the story of our journey. Perhaps the hardest lesson that I'm attempting to incorporate into my life in this desert wandering is that I can't fairly judge others for how they respond to the opportunities provided to them by life. Nor should I harshly judge myself. Ultimately, I believe that we each generally do the best we can with what we've got. I also believe that we can each continue to grow.

Bishop Gumbleton did the best he could when he sat across from me in his office twenty-plus years ago as I asked for his support. We both did the best we could. But his best, I felt, was not good enough for me and my needs. And he felt there was nothing more he could do for me.

I lost track of Bishop Gumbleton when I left Detroit in 1976, but apparently he decided that he needed to do better for others than he had been able to do for me. He too had a hunger that drove him to stretch beyond his boundaries of comfort in search of new ways to understand homosexuality.

A couple of years ago, I learned that the bishop was courageously speaking out in behalf of gay people and those with AIDS. He was pictured in national Catholic newspapers celebrating Mass for Dignity in a rainbow miter. He was quoted widely for his bold challenge to the Church to be more loving in its response to gay people. He was leading workshops for clergy and religious on providing a more compassionate response to the gay community, and he was working closely with Sister Jeannine Gramick and Father Bob Nugent at New Ways Ministry, an unsanctioned Catholic outreach to gay men, lesbians, and bisexuals.

When I read of his work, I sent him a letter of congratulations and encouragement. Guessing that he might not remember me after those many years, I reintroduced myself and applauded the bishop for his powerful and very important witness. I have met many gay Catholics in my life who have struggled desperately to reconcile their religion with their sexual orientation. For those gay, lesbian, and bisexual people, in particular, I enthusiastically thanked Bishop Gumbleton.

The bishop replied:

"It was good to hear from you after such a long absence. I'm happy to know you are doing well.

"When I reflect on your experience in Detroit at *The Michigan Catholic,* I now have a better sense of how very, very difficult it must have been for you. Truly you were ahead of your time in calling for understanding for the gay community. I am sure those days were filled with frustration and loneliness. I'm personally grateful that you persevered.

"My affiliation with New Ways Ministry and my experience in working with HIV-positive and PWAs [People with AIDS] have opened my eyes. Know that I will continue to do all that I can to work for justice and understanding for the homosexual community.

"Keep me in your prayers and I'll be praying for you, too."

I was delighted to receive his letter. But I was also very curious. What prompted the bishop to let go of the caution he showed me and to become a role model for his peers? How did he get involved with New Ways Ministry? I called him to find out.

"I was totally unhelpful and insensitive to you," the bishop said when he reflected on our meeting in 1974. "I didn't know anything about homosexuality. I grew up with a fear of asking questions about sex."

"Education is the key. That's why I fasted," I said. "Lots of clergy called me and said, 'They don't teach about sex in seminary. How are we supposed to know about this?' "

"I'm glad they called you. Some of us entered seminary after eighth grade," the bishop said. "I was embarrassed to ask questions."

"Was it true, as I heard, that you hadn't really written the letter that ended my hunger fast?" I asked him.

Graciously and humbly he acknowledged that he had indeed written the letter. "I recall writing it, but I'm sure I heard from [Monsignor] Clem Kern. I'm sure I had his encouragement.

"But I wish I had done more," he added. "I have sad feelings of failure about what happened to you. We failed you. It was a real loss to the newspaper and to the diocese."

His kind words touched me very deeply.

Bishop Gumbleton then explained that my civil rights case with the diocese gnawed at him for many years. He started speaking up about discrimination against homosexuals, separating the issue of justice from that of sexual morality.

"Then I began doing some reading," he said. He found John McNeill's book *The Church and the Homosexual*[13] and Father Tony Kosnik's *Human Sexuality: New Directions in Catholic Thought*[14] particularly helpful. He also became familiar with the work of Dignity and of New Ways Ministry. Because of his reputation as an advocate for social justice issues, he was asked to serve on the board of St. Francis House, an AIDS hospice in Florida.

And then it got personal.

"My younger brother Dan sent a letter to every member of the family telling us that he was gay," the bishop said. "I was angry. I thought, 'What if this comes out in the open? What's this going to do to me?' "

"That's a pretty normal response," I said.

"It was a lot easier to deal with when it was in someone else's family," Bishop Gumbleton replied with a knowing laugh. "I had no problem responding to other people's issues. But I couldn't respond to his letter."

The bishop recalls then doing more reading and thinking as he worked to sort out his feelings. He also recalls being touched by the lives of two people with whom he worked.

"The board of Pax Christi [a Catholic peace group] was having this incredible debate about whether or not to take a position on gay civil rights," he explained. "The next morning, Mike, one of the board members, came out to the group and talked to us about how it felt to sit through the debate. People were moved. They liked and admired him. We developed a policy statement."

While working with St. Francis House in Tampa, the bishop met Olga, the elderly Cuban-born mother of a gay man who died of AIDS. Olga didn't care much about the moral debates on homosexuality. She cared about her son.

"I have two sons," she told the bishop. "One is in heaven and one is on earth."

"She wasn't going to reject him because he was gay or because he had AIDS," he told me. "She was proud of him."

One night, not long after, the bishop dropped in on his eighty-six-year-old mother, who lived near his parish in Detroit.

"We were sitting on the back porch," Bishop Gumbleton said, "and my mother looked at me and asked, 'Tom, is your brother Dan going to hell?'

"She loved her son but it was weighing on her mind. She needed to hear from me what she knew to be true in her own heart.

" 'No, of course not, Mom,' I said, 'Dan is not going to go to hell. God made Dan the way he is.' "

I congratulated him on his response.

"I said it with conviction," the bishop replied. "I *believe* it."

"What you're doing today on behalf of gay people is the work of God," I said.

"I know that," he answered. "I only wish that I had done a better job with you."

"We both did the best we could," I said.

Today, we're both doing better.

Twenty-some years ago, I wanted something very different from the bishop than I got during our recent telephone conversation. In 1974, I wanted his approval and I wanted him to defend me. Fortunately for me, he could do neither. As a result, I learned to give myself approval and I learned to defend myself.

Twenty-some years ago, I wanted the bishop to embrace me. The embrace I experienced recently was not the one I wanted in 1974. It was better. It was an embrace *with* Tom and not *from* the bishop.

The conversation we had on the telephone was deeply healing for both of us. To the casual eye, a former Catholic gay man and a heterosexual bishop crossed paths briefly and reminisced on their past. For me, two spiritual pilgrims met in the desert again, celebrated their common goal, hugged each other in affirmation, and continued on their journeys grateful to know the other was out there somewhere.

10

ABOUT
ASSESSING THE OPTIONS

Have you ever sat in an airport, studied another passenger, and wondered, "What's that person's life like?"

I do it all the time, not just in airports, but also while sitting in traffic, walking on the beach, and running through the park. I'm real curious as to how others are different from or the same as me, not so much in how they look, but more in how they *feel*.

"Are they happy being who they are? What, if anything, about their life would they change?"

It occurs to me that other people may look at me and wonder the same, particularly if they know that I'm gay.

As I hope is true for each of them, I wouldn't want to be anyone other than me. That's not to say that I wouldn't like to have a more muscular torso, or perhaps a stronger chin, but I love being *who* and *what* I am. I love being gay. And though there are things I would probably go back and do differently, I have no regrets about my life as a gay man. In the words of my good friend Monty, my life's been "pretty wonderful."

Unfortunately, because of the nature of my work, not enough people hear me say this to the degree to which I'd like it known. One of the personal drawbacks of my work is that my effectiveness in creating allies is directly related to my ability to communicate the pain and isolation that usually accompany growing up gay, lesbian, or bisexual. When people understand the oppression we face, they're more inclined to see the need for policies that protect and behaviors that support us. But they often get an incomplete picture.

I've always hoped that members of my audience were able to experience my joy as a gay man from my words and manner, and I've regretted not having the time and opportunity to speak more extensively about how happy I am with my life.

Ray and I frequently do take the time to reflect on how grateful we are for our lives. Given the amount of work-related traveling we're both required to do, we make sure to say often that should either of us die unexpectedly, we'd do so feeling we'd lived a richly satisfying life. "No regrets," we say.

Now, clearly, I'd liked to have grown up in a home that understood and encouraged me, gone to schools that acknowledged and supported me, and worshipped in a Church that loved and honored me for being the special expression of divinity that I am.

And, yes, I spent the first twenty-six years of my life in terror of being discovered. I've been verbally abused and physically threatened because of my sexual orientation. I was fired from a job I loved because I'm gay. And I've experienced more loss of friends than any person my age should be expected to suffer.

But if I hadn't been gay, I might never have seen Larry Wald promenade down Commercial Street in Provincetown, Massachusetts, in his award-winning carnival gown of 1,800-plus Barbie dolls, all of whom he'd named. Nor might I have been able to laugh and enjoy Larry's brilliant whimsy because my sense of masculinity could have been too threatened. Nor would I have watched this parade, or any other, with Ray Struble lovingly at my side.

If I hadn't been gay, I might never have stood cheering, tears rolling down my cheeks, as George Hearn belted out "I Am What I Am" to a packed gay house at the Boston premiere of *La Cage aux Folles*. Nor might I have known the great satisfaction of proclaiming the same truth at the risk of losing things once held precious. Nor might I ever have met so many other marvelous brave souls whose bold celebration of self inspired my daring.

If I hadn't been gay, I might never have shaken my head in grateful awe as I watched uniformed lesbian, bisexual, and gay New York City cops proudly stride past the Stonewall bar during the Gay Pride parade, preceded by the NYPD Marching Band. Nor might I have been able to truly understand the power of the people to bring about such significant social change. Nor might I have stood next to a Latina couple of twenty-three years, in front of an Asian man, an Indian woman, and a black transsexual, and felt such solidarity as together we cheered this historic event.

I celebrate having been born gay because of the beautiful kaleidoscope life to which it has exposed me, the important journey of personal growth it's required me to make, and the incredible experience of love and happiness it has brought me.

And it's not *despite* the oppression I have faced as a gay man, but *because of it,* that I've had the wonderful opportunity to live my life so honestly and therefore so joyfully. Being gay has required and rewarded a life lived *deliberately.*

In this regard, Henry David Thoreau summed up my feelings well.

"I went to the woods because I wished to live deliberately, to front only the essential facts of life, and see if I could not learn what it had to teach, and not, when I came to die, discover that I had not lived."

Those powerfully appropriate words from *Walden* are displayed at Thoreau's cabin site in the woods of Walden Pond. At age twenty-eight, this Harvard-educated disciple of Ralph Waldo Emerson voluntarily withdrew from his privileged and convenient life in Concord, Massachusetts, in order to discern for himself what in life was truly essential. For two years he lived alone in a one-room cabin of his own construction.

Inspired by, and identifying with, his actions and creed, Ray and I would frequently pack up the dog, out-of-town guests, a thermos of coffee, and a pocketful of apples and trek out to Thoreau's sanctuary to pay homage.

"Be sure to pick up a stone along the way," I would advise our friends. "Make it something that speaks to you."

Upon our arrival, my instructions became clear. There, by the site of his cabin, was a large mound of stones, or cairn, created by other pilgrims as a monument to Thoreau's philosophy.

Though we've since moved a long distance from Walden Pond, we continue to be motivated by Thoreau's words and to celebrate the similarities between our lives and his. We're not living in a one-room cabin, but as gay men we're certainly fronting the essential facts of life and are learning what it has to teach us.

Accordingly, we maintain a cairn of our own. Made not of stones but of the buttons, badges, name tags, pins, and other memorabilia we've picked up along the way, it gives testimony to our gay journey in the "wilderness." Piled high in an old wooden bowl in my office, this mound of tin, plastic, and paper provides evidence of why we have no regrets about our lives as gay men.

"Dignity" is written on some of the earliest buttons and badges collected on our path. Its name represents our first departure from the privileges and conveniences of the world for the sake of a life lived deliberately. It was in this young organization of gay Catholics that Ray and I found each other and an important bridge between our faith and our lives. Both joyous and exhilarating, our years in the group also mark an extraordinarily challenging time for us.

I recall, for instance, sitting frightened but determined in an inner-city church in Detroit in 1974, at a Mass of Solidarity in support of my civil rights case with *The Michigan Catholic* newspaper. Hundreds of invitations were sent by Dignity to local Catholic priests and religious to join us, but only a small handful of brave souls came.

My best friend from high school, Henry Grix, took his place as a straight ally next to me in the front pew. Police officers milled around outside in anticipation of conflict. The tension in the church was gradually eased by the repeated singing of the refrain "They will know we are Christians by our love." But we then gasped in horror and outrage as members of Catholics United for the Faith rushed the altar and unfurled their large banner that proclaimed: A MORAL WRONG CAN NEVER BE A CIVIL RIGHT. A struggle ensued as a couple of gay Vietnam veterans who served as our ushers grabbed the banner and escorted the extremist group's demonstrators out of church.

It was through a number of experiences such as this that I was forced to confront a variety of essential questions about my spirituality and sexuality that I might never have faced as a heterosexual male worshipping inconspicuously in a welcoming parish.

"Am I, as a homosexual, truly made in the image and likeness of God?" I asked myself at age twenty-six. "Can the genital expression of my gay sexuality be spiritual?" "Should I expect ever to feel welcome and nurtured in this institution?" My answers to those queries dramatically changed the direction of my life by bolstering my confidence as a gay man, intensifying my faith, and eventually leading me out of the church.

Painful and unsettling as it was, I'm very grateful for the necessity of seriously challenging my beliefs. Rejection by the institutional church forced me to decide what elements of my faith were essential and what could be discarded. Had I experienced no conflict with the hierarchy of my religion, I might never have bothered to seriously consider what I professed to be universal truth.

"Anita Bryant Sucks Oranges" reads another of our earliest buttons in the wooden bowl. Along with the one that says, "A Day Without Human Rights Is Like a Day Without Sunshine," it speaks to me of the experience of being publicly scorned and rejected by the majority of society because I'm gay, but not being personally defeated as a result of it. Instead, I was empowered.

Anita Bryant, the celebrated spokesperson for the orange juice industry, assumed to speak as God's representative in Dade County, Florida, in 1977. The media presented images of her praying with her family for strength in her fight to "Save Our Children" from the threat of homosexuality. She was joined in her crusade by the local Catholic bishop, who publicly announced that he would go to jail rather than hire a homosexual.

Gay, lesbian, and bisexual people rallied valiantly across the country by boycotting orange juice, sending donations, and volunteering time to defeat the vicious, demeaning public campaign against us. And the whole world watched as the voters went to the polls to decide the fate of our civil rights.

The results dominated the headlines of newspapers in every U.S. city. Previously granted protections against discrimination based on sexual orientation had been rescinded.

As a privileged, white, middle-class male, I had little training in fighting for status in the court of public opinion. I was initially hurt, angry, sad, and depressed. But, I soon discovered, I wasn't destroyed. In fact, I became more determined than ever to affirm myself as a gay man, and I learned that far from being a "wus," I was a warrior. The Dade County battle, coupled with my own civil rights struggle with the church, forced me to step forward and address more basic issues of life.

"Do I need the approval of others to be happy?" "Does 'majority rule' mean justice prevails?" "What in life is worth fighting for?"

Ultimately, I decided with exhilaration that I could live a very happy and fulfilled life even if I was feared and hated by the majority of people. That is an enormously significant lesson. One of the greatest gifts of my journey as a gay man has been discovering that what I think of myself is far more important than what others think of me.

My value and my right to happiness cannot and will not be determined by a popular referendum, by an executive order, or by a majority vote of the Supreme Court. I'm not sure I would have learned that liberating lesson had I not experienced the personal attack and denial of my rights that occurred in the Dade County battle.

Also in our wooden bowl are membership cards to the National Organization for Women (NOW), Amnesty International, Planned Parenthood, Bread for the World, Habitat for Humanity, the ACLU, and People for the American Way, among others. These call to mind another important insight gained from my fights against anti-gay bias. I am not alone on my journey.

One of the bonuses of being in an oppressed minority is the entrée it can provide into the minds and hearts of other special people living in the woods. When I came into touch with the personal impact of rejection, it enabled me to better understand and respond to the feelings of others who face discrimination for different reasons. They in turn, in learning of my journey, have often let down their defenses and welcomed me into the unique beauty of their worlds. The friendships that I have created with these fellow travelers are among the richest and most rewarding of my life.

Still other political buttons in the pile tell the inspiring stories of gay friends who have boldly stepped forward to challenge the inequalities in our lives. Some of them did so by running for political office in the early days of the movement. Among the dozens of these buttons, "Elaine Noble for U.S. Senate" is one of my favorites. It recalls one of my early role models and my experience with the courage and determination that can mark the life of a lesbian, bisexual, gay, or transgender person.

As the first openly gay representative elected to a state house, Elaine saw no reason why she shouldn't also be the first self-affirmed lesbian in the U.S. Senate. In 1978 she announced her bid to be the Democratic challenger to Republican incumbent Senator Ed Brooke of Massachusetts. Political analysts, including Speaker of the House Tip O'Neill, applauded her daring. Few, however, thought she could win. She was unknown outside of Boston and she was a lesbian.

It was my honor to drive this feisty coal miner's daughter across the state to meet the voters.

"Hi there," she said with her beautiful smile, her hand outstretched to the firefighters in a remote town in the western corner of the commonwealth. "I'm Elaine Noble. I'm running for U.S. Senate and I'd like your vote. I'd also like to take a ride down that pole. Would that be okay?"

They, like most others, were immediately charmed, returning her smile with ones of their own. As I recall, though, we weren't allowed to slide down the pole. But we did get hearty handshakes and the promise they'd consider her candidacy.

The most famous lesbian in the country at the time had chutzpah that I admired and that inspired me. Elaine's strength, in my young gay eyes, came from her daring to be herself, unashamed, with conviction, dignity, a nondefensive posture, and a great sense of humor.

"Someone spray-painted the word 'Lebanese' across the side of my car," she told her audiences with a chuckle. "Would someone please help that person learn to spell?"

Though she lost the primary to Paul Tsongas, Elaine, and her contemporary, Allan Spear in the Minnesota state senate, blazed a trail in politics that helped prepare the way for other gay, lesbian, and bisexual people with a vision of public service.

I have lots of other cherished political buttons too, like those for well-known U.S. Representatives Gerry Studds and Barney Frank, for friends who ran and didn't win, and for great organizations like the Gay and Lesbian Victory Fund that formed to get our people elected. Each reflects for me the inspiring struggle of gay people who have dared to front ugly opposition for the sake of equal representation. (One day soon, Ray and I will have a button for an openly gay U.S. senator to proudly place in the collection. And what a story that will be!)

There are many other powerful stories of determination represented by buttons in our bowl, and not all are about politicians. "Another Friend of Charlie Howard," for instance, painfully recalls the death of a young gay man who drowned after being thrown over a bridge in Bangor, Maine, by teenage bullies. But the button also reminds me of Charlie's, and other young gay people's, courage, stamina, and hope for the future.

I shudder thinking about what it would be like to wake up every day and prepare to go into a school where I knew I would be emotionally and physically abused because I was perceived as being a "sissy," "fairy," "punk," or "wus." Luckily, I passed for straight in high school and was spared open hostility, because I didn't have the confidence at the time to name myself. But the young men and women today who can't pass or who are bold enough to "sing their songs" aren't so fortunate. They often become the targets of those who are threatened by difference.

Nevertheless, the majority of these "sissy" boys and "dykish" girls keep getting out of bed each morning knowing they probably will be mocked that day, keep getting dressed knowing they may be spat upon, keep going to class knowing other kids may not want to sit near them, keep going to the restroom knowing that it's an opportunity for insecure classmates to have their fun with them.

Some gay youths, like Jamie Nabozny, end up in the hospital after continued physical abuse in school. Others, like Charlie Howard, end up dead. Despite it all, however, the majority of gay, lesbian, bisexual, and transgender youths refuse to be defeated for life by the wretched acts of cowardly gay-bashers. Instead, they are strengthened by the challenges and they maintain their hope for the future. Their courage makes a mockery of the beliefs of people such as Lieutenant Colonel Oliver North, who insists that if gay men are allowed to serve in the military, "no *real* man will ever enlist again."

Had I not been gay, I might never have asked myself, "What makes a man a man?" I might have relied instead upon the right-wing talk show host to define it for me, or gleaned my role models from adventure films and advertising campaigns. But because I am gay, and know of people such as Charlie Howard, I have been forced to evaluate society's and my standards of manliness, and to decide for myself the characteristics of, and the importance of being, a *real* man or a *real* woman.

Being gay has also provided me with some other wonderful personal gay male role models. These include people such as Frank Kameny, who took on the U.S. government over the issue of security clearances; Troy Perry, who challenged the National Council of Churches to recognize his gay-friendly religious denomination; Lenny Matlovich, who led the charge against the homophobic exclusionary clause of the Armed Forces; and Tom Waddell, who ended up losing his home as a result of his battle with the U.S. Olympic Committee to create safe space for gay athletes.

These individuals, and so many others like them, inspired me by their bold, confident expressions of self in the face of enormous opposition. In them and in my long list of gay, lesbian, and bisexual role models, I witness courage, vulnerability, honesty, vision, and strength of conviction. Regrettably, sometimes I have become most aware of some gay people's great stature at the time of their death.

"Someone I Love Has AIDS," "The Names Project," and "Imagine, Demand, and Work for a Cure": these buttons, and the many others like them in the bowl, remind me not only of the legion of heroic friends lost but also of the many important lessons learned as a result of our herculean battle against the human immunodeficiency virus (HIV).

Horrible nightmare that it is for us all, HIV forged a dynamic, empowered community among gay, lesbian, and bisexual people and enabled us to see clearly how brave, determined, generous, and thoroughly decent we are. Thousands and thousands of us have volunteered our time, donated our resources, and put our lives on the line to care for our own, to find a cure, and to get the respectful attention of a frightened world.

HIV and AIDS have also forced us to confront at an early age the essential letting go that is required in this life, to decide our beliefs about a life hereafter, and to come to terms with our own mortality.

"Why is life so unfair?" "Where do others go when they leave me?" and "Am I prepared to die?" are not necessarily questions I would have faced by age thirty-three had I been born heterosexual. They are certainly issues I could probably have avoided at nineteen. Not so for most gay kids today. They know that while AIDS is a public health crisis that affects everyone, it casts a particularly long shadow over their lives.

Strange as it might be to imagine, though, my buddy Sam said AIDS was the best thing that ever happened to him. When we were brought together by the AIDS Action Committee in Boston, Sam was pretty healthy looking. He lived at home with his mom and sister, raised calla lilies and orchids in his own greenhouse, and had only recently quit his job as a florist.

He explained that he hadn't thought much about what was important in life until he got his diagnosis. Then, he said, he started to really appreciate each and every day. He began to truly savor the food we shared, the feel of the sun on his face, the sound of his mother's laughter, the sight of his flowers blooming, and the many complex thoughts that entered his head.

"Do you think there's a God?" he asked me. "Have I lived a good life?" "What's heaven like?" "If my Dad was alive, would he be proud of me?" "What have I accomplished?"

As Sam asked his questions, I asked the same of myself. As he tasted the food, felt the sun, listened to the sound of laughter, and remarked at the delicate beauty of his flowers, I did too. I would love to say that, in honor of Sam, I continue to relish every moment of every day, but regrettably I don't. Nevertheless, I'm much more conscious of the need to do so than before I met him. So too, I suspect, are most people who are HIV-positive or who love someone who is.

When Sam died, his family, as he had instructed, asked me to give the eulogy at his funeral. However, they added, "Please don't tell anyone that he was gay or how he died." By using the metaphor of flowers, I was able to both accommodate their sad request and underscore for those gathered what a "wonderfully unique bloom" Sam had been, but I did so with enormously conflicted feelings and with the resolve that my life would never be so denied.

When Mark, my second buddy, died, I was confronted with a similar request for duplicity from the family. In a small Jewish cemetery off a dirt road in rural Maine, hundreds of miles from his beloved life of theater and opera in Manhattan, Mark's body was laid to rest, shrouded in mystery.

"Were you a friend of Mark's?" asked an older woman as Ray and I took our seats for the memorial service.

"Yes," whispered Ray, hoping that would be all he was asked to say.

"How did he die?" she asked.

"I don't know," he answered, feeling completely foolish but aware of the family's request.

"Did I do okay?" he asked me later.

"You did just fine," I said. "What choice did you have?"

After family members had all bid their farewells, a small group of what I assumed were gay male friends huddled together around the burial site, their black trench coats shielding them from others and the late summer rain. Who exactly they were and the particulars of what they were whispering to each other and to Mark are unknown to me, but their stories and words would undoubtedly be familiar.

Regrettably, they left before Ray and I got the chance to introduce ourselves, but my guess is that we have since unknowingly bumped elbows in Washington, D.C., while searching for Mark's panel among the others displayed in the AIDS Memorial Quilt. And it is in standing or kneeling before the three-by-six-foot handmade testimonies of this great national treasure that we all take comfort in knowing that Mark, Sam, and the thousands of others like them have not lived with no one knowing who they were or how they died.

It's also possible that I've bumped the elbows of Mark's New York friends while parading around the White House during the 1979, 1987, or 1993 March on Washington. I did so with hundreds of thousands of other gay, lesbian, bisexual, transgender, and heterosexual people at those times. Some truly handsome pins and buttons in the bowl give witness to those exhilarating moments in my life.

One hundred thousand people from all over America came by every mode of transportation to the nation's capital for the first march, in 1979, to protest against anti-gay discrimination and to proclaim, "We are everywhere and we shall be free." President Jimmy Carter was in the White House then, Anita Bryant was still savoring her victory, Harvey Milk had recently been assassinated, Gerry Studds had yet to come out, and "Ayds" was popularly known as a weight-loss pill.

When we marchers saw how many of us there were on subway platforms, in line at restaurants, and spread across the Great Mall, we laughed with surprise, delighted in our diversity, and thoroughly relished our brief but powerful moment in the sun.

Eight years later, we came back. Ronald Reagan was in the White House and thousands of those who had marched with us in 1979 were now dead. "Shame, shame, shame," we chanted as we proceeded down Pennsylvania Avenue. We were an angrier group than before, sobered by the plague, but nevertheless more sure of ourselves. The numbers in attendance had swelled to several hundred thousand, as we veterans of the first march had inspired excited interest among our family and friends. Ray and I walked with our brothers Tommy and David. Also with us was my high school friend, Henry Grix, now a budding self-identified gay man.

When we once again returned to Washington six years later, we claimed six hundred thousand in attendance. Gay, lesbian, and bisexual military veterans led our march amid proud and encouraging cheers of support. Bill Clinton was in the White House and AIDS had stolen over two hundred thousand American lives. Bobby Jaston was one of those.

Bobby was David's best friend. They trained together as New York Air flight attendants. He was a handsome young man with an infectious smile, mischievous big brown eyes, and a robust playfulness. Although we were ever-hopeful of beating the odds, Bobby's death made David's own diagnosis more real and threatening to all of us.

Teary-eyed, we accompanied our brother as he presented Bobby's panel for inclusion in the quilt, a small display of which coincided with the march. The image of Ray and David holding one another as they wept at the quilt is another sacred memory captured in our cairn by the button, "The Quilt. See It and Understand."

Back at the march, it took hours before the last contingent could leave the starting point for the rally site, at which Gerry Studds was speaking. Along the route, there was the customary crop of well-worn banners warning of fire and brimstone, but they were outnumbered by the thousands of people cheering as each group representing a state or organization passed by.

Ray and I walked with the AIDS Action Committee. Tommy was their communications director and also coordinated their march. David, a long-time volunteer with the group, was proudly holding one of their multicolored flags.

Our friends Carol Dopp and Pam Wilson found us, and joined in with the large group of other straight allies with whom they had connected. My gay friend Henry walked hand in hand with Howard Israel, whom he'd met at the march in 1987 and has been with ever since.

As anyone who, like Henry, was present for these national gatherings, for the Gay Games, for local pride parades, or even for a Mass of Solidarity can tell us, these events can change one's life forever. There is an indescribable feeling of self-actualization that comes from participating in one's own liberation. Being plunged into the happy and angry tears, defiant screams, exuberant cheers, knowing smiles, hearty laughs, and the wise silence of fellow soldiers can baptize you into a new world of self-determination. Awakened or renewed, men and women feel themselves much less the victims and much more the scripters of their own destinies.

Proof of this comes in the form of one of the last groups to enter the Mall in 1993. LESBIAN, BISEXUAL, AND GAY UNITED EMPLOYEES (LEAGUE) AT AT&T announced their banner. Beneath it proudly marched those in engineering, sales, public relations, maintenance, advertising, government relations, and production, among other endeavors. As one of their buttons in our wooden bowl informs us, "It's Great 2B Gay at AT&T."

This grandparent of all gay business resource groups was created as a direct result of the 1987 March on Washington. Some AT&T employees from Denver attended that gathering, were deeply touched and energized as a result, and returned home determined to come out at work. To support themselves and others in that effort, they started the first chapter of LEAGUE.

Being a part of this pioneering effort has been a source of enormous joy and pride in my life. Participating in the education of heterosexual business people, as well as those outside of corporate America, has filled my days in the woods with the excitement of knowing I am making a difference in the world as an openly gay man. That is another big reason I have no regrets about my life.

And as other buttons, pins, and badges in our bowl help say, it's not just the challenging issues of my life that make me glad that I was born gay. It's also the pure joy that I have experienced as a result of my sexual orientation.

"Are We Having Fun Yet?" asks one button. Speaking only for myself, I'm having *great* fun, and have since I first came out. Larry Wald with his Barbie doll gown is only one of a thousand gay, lesbian, bisexual, and transgender people I have met on my journey who have brought me joy and laughter with their whimsical insights on life and their playful expressions of self.

Rita Mae Brown's description of the Christmas pageant in *Rubyfruit Jungle*[1] made me laugh so hard I woke up the house. Armistead Maupin's *Tales of the City*[2] provided a family of delightfully crazy gay-positive friends I cried over departing as I finished the series. The Kids in the Hall, Kate Clinton, Funny Gay Males, RuPaul, Harvey Fierstein, Suzanne Westenhoefer, Lynn Lavner, Paul Rudnick, and Quentin Crisp, among so many others, allow me to constantly savor the delights of gay sensibility.

I also enjoy incredible satisfaction as a gay man being mesmerized by the Tony Award–winning performance of Cherry Jones as *The Heiress,* being thrilled by the Pulitzer Prize–winning writing of Tony Kushner in *Angels in America,* and being captivated by the Grammy Award–winning singing and songwriting of Tracy Chapman. I love the experience of participating in the brilliant creativity of openly gay, lesbian, and bisexual artists and professionals. Greg Louganis, Martina Navratilova, Keith Haring, k. d. lang, David Hockney, Tom Hulce, Alice Walker, Rudy Galindo, Philip Johnson, Sir Ian McKellen, James Baldwin, Bob Paris, Melissa Etheridge, David Geffen, Terrence McNally, Audre Lorde, Edmund White, and Marlon Riggs are among the long list of those whose accomplishments fill me with great pride.

Our "Free Hugs" button reminds me of the enormous joy I get in being able as a gay man to comfortably hug, kiss, and say "I love you" to my lesbian and gay friends, as well as to my female and male heterosexual allies. Gay, lesbian, bisexual, and transgender people have been pioneers in challenging the artificial and restrictive cultural boundaries of gender roles. Freed of social convention and approval, we have learned to reach out and touch consensually those of both genders. In so doing, we've not only unshackled our own feelings of affection but also helped liberate others to do the same.

My dad, for instance, like most other men I know, grew up fearing that intimate expression between men was inappropriate. Yet, he learned from his two gay sons and gay son-in-law that it was not only okay to hug, kiss, and say "I love you" to another man, but that it was the most natural and appropriate expression of affection and love. I'm so glad to have been able to share with him that wonderful gift of my life before he died. So too, I think, was he.

"I Like Boys," boldly announces one oversize button. More accurately, it should read, "I Love Men." One very important reason that I not only have no regrets about being gay but thank God for the life I've been given is that I love the male body. I love masculinity (not "supermachismo"). And I love sex with another man. Furthermore, I'm crazy about Ray Struble and if I weren't gay, I wouldn't be able to spend my life in a loving, sexual union with him. How intolerably sad that would make me.

"Honorary Lesbian" is an actual title I've been given but not a button that I've yet found. When I do, though, I'll quickly add it to our cairn because I *love* lesbians. Among my lesbian and heterosexual feminist friends, I find people who embrace their womanhood free of limiting cultural conventions. In their presence, therefore, I experience a whole person, unafraid to tap both their feminine and masculine natures. I, in turn, then feel free to do the same.

Being born a gay person has created for me a wonderful opportunity for a very interesting, challenging, and rewarding life. It doesn't guarantee anything, nor does it eliminate any significant possibilities. There is pain and sadness in the life of most gay people because there is pain and sadness in all of life. But out of that suffering can come extraordinary strength and insights that will serve us all well. There is also the option for amazing love and joy in the life journeys of gay, lesbian, and bisexual people. It's a matter of being open to it.

There's no one right way to be gay in the world. There's no one gay way to act, think, feel, pray, work, love, or have sex. The direction of our lives, as is true for all human beings, is best left to the voice within. If we listen to that voice, we will live deliberately, and when we die we will know that we have fully lived. What more could one want?

SOURCES

CHAPTER ONE
ABOUT FITTING INTO THE GAY COMMUNITY

1. I know that gay, lesbian, and bisexual are words with different meanings to different people. Gay usually, but not exclusively, refers to homosexual men; lesbian refers to homosexual women; bisexual refers to men and women who feel erotic/affectional attraction to both genders. Though all three groups of people experience discrimination because of their sexual orientations, each group has different experiences with self-discovery, with how each conceptualizes and expresses sexuality, and with prejudice. And within each group there is diversity in attitudes and experiences. I will use, as often as possible, all three words together in a sentence. But most people appreciate how cumbersome always using all three words can be for the writer and the reader. For that reason, the word gay, for lack of a more personally acceptable word, is employed as a shorthand reference to gay men, lesbian women, and bisexual people. I also, as often as possible, use gay, lesbian, and bisexual as adjectives rather than as nouns to underscore that sexual orientation is a part of who we are, as are race and gender, but not all of who we are. Finally, I will often include the word transgender to acknowledge the oppression shared with those persons discriminated against because of their gender role or gender identity.

2. Urvashi Vaid, *Virtual Equality: The Mainstreaming of Gay and Lesbian Liberation* (New York: Anchor Books, 1995).

3. Andrew Sullivan, *Virtually Normal: An Argument About Homosexuality:* (New York: Alfred A. Knopf, 1995).

4. Bruce Bawer, *A Place at the Table: The Gay Individual in American Society* (New York: Poseidon Press, 1993).

5. Michelangelo Signorile, *Queer in America: Sex, the Media, and the Closets of Power* (New York: Random House, 1993).

6. Melody Beattie, *Codependent No More: How to Stop Controlling Others and Start Caring for Yourself* (New York: Harper/Hazelden, 1987).

Sources

CHAPTER TWO
ABOUT THE MAN ON THE PLANE

1. Vivienne Cass, "Homosexual Identity Formation: A Theoretical Model," *Journal of Homosexuality 4,* no. 3 (Spring 1979).

CHAPTER THREE
ABOUT SEXUALITY

1. Sexuality Information and Education Council of the United States (SIECUS), Position Statement on Sexuality Issues (New York, 1995).

2. John Rechy, *The Sexual Outlaw: A Documentary,* rev. ed. (New York: Grove/Atlantic, 1984).

3. Anthony Kosnik, et al., *Human Sexuality, New Directions in American Catholic Thought: A Study Commissioned by the Catholic Theological Society of America* (New York: Paulist Press, 1977), pp. 82, 92.

CHAPTER FOUR
ABOUT LOVE AND MARRIAGE

1. Ruth 1:16–17 New American Bible.

2. On December 3, 1996, Hawaii Circuit Judge Kevin Chang ruled in *Baehr v. Miike* that the state failed to show a "compelling state interest" in denying marriage licenses to gay couples. The suit challenging Hawaii's same-sex marriage ban was filed in 1991 by three gay couples: Joe Melillo and Pat Lagon, Tammy Rodrigues and Antoinette Pregil, and Ninia Baehr and Genora Dancel. Hawaii thus became the first state in the nation to officially recognize gay and lesbian marriages. The state has appealed Judge Chang's decision to the state Supreme Court. An earlier favorable ruling by that court on the matter strongly suggests it will uphold Judge Chang's decision. A final decision by the court is expected in 1998. Because the case involves state and not federal rights, it cannot be appealed to the U.S. Supreme Court.

3. On September 18, 1996, President Bill Clinton signed into law the Defense of Marriage Act (DOMA), which: (1) confines federal recognition of marriage to a union between a man and a woman, and (2) allows states to deny recognition to a same-sex marriage from another state.

4. Lambda Legal Defense and Education Fund, Marriage Project information material, New York, 1996.

5. Ibid.

6. Deb Price, "History Reminds Us That We Should Adopt a Vow of Tolerance Regarding Marriage," *The Detroit News*, April 14, 1995.

7. Evan Wolfson, *Lambda Update* 13, no. 3 (Fall 1996).

8. Virginia Code Ann. §20–57.

9. Gertrude Stein.

10. Gertrude Stein, *Three Lives: Stories of the Good Anna, Melanctha, and the Gentle Lena* (New York: Grafton Press, 1909).

11. Alice B. Toklas, *What Is Remembered* (London: Michael Joseph, 1963).

CHAPTER FIVE
ABOUT THE WORKPLACE

1. Wall Street Project, "The Equality Principles on Sexual Orientation" (see Resources, "Political and Work-Related").

2. Howard Tharsing, V Management's "Lavender Screen Test" (see Resources, "Political and Work-Related").

CHAPTER SIX
ABOUT OUR FAMILIES

1. Richard Pillard and J.D. Weinrich, "Evidence of Familial Nature of Male Homosexuality," *Archives of General Psychiatry* 43 (1986), pp. 808–812.

CHAPTER SEVEN
ABOUT OUR GAY, LESBIAN AND BISEXUAL YOUTH

1. James Brooke, "To Be Young, Gay and Going to High School in Utah," *New York Times*, February 28, 1996, B8.

2. Associated Press, "Gay Student Clubs in Utah Face a Ban," *New York Times*, April 19, 1996, A22.

3. Jamie Nabozny was awarded $900,000 on November 20, 1996, in an out-of-court settlement after a Federal court jury found the principal of his middle school and the principal and vice principal of his high school liable for failing to protect him from repeated abuse by other students. Nabozny had filed suit against the Ashland, Wisconsin, school district and school administrators. The jury found the school district as a whole was not liable.

4. Dawn Terry, "Suit Says Schools Failed to Protect a Gay Student," *New York Times,* March 29, 1996, A14.

5. Commonwealth of Massachusetts, H.R. 3353, *An Act to Prohibit Discrimination Against Students in Public Schools on the Basis of Sexual Orientation* (1993).

CHAPTER EIGHT
ABOUT OUR ALLIES

1. Cracker Barrel Old Country Store, Inc., a fast-growing chain of restaurants with over fourteen thousand employees in sixteen states, announced in January 1991 a new employment policy that bars people "whose sexual preferences fail to demonstrate normal heterosexual values, which have been the foundation of families in our society." At least eleven gay and lesbian employees were summarily fired. In response to media coverage and protests, the policy was rescinded, but the company never rehired the dismissed employees. Instead, it defended its anti-gay policy by saying it was "a well-intentioned overreaction to the perceived values of our customers and their comfort levels with these individuals." A boycott of the restaurant chain is being observed by consumers who want a good-faith effort from Cracker Barrel to address and remedy the damage it did.

2. John F. Kennedy, *Profiles in Courage* (New York: Harper, 1956).

3. Gregory Herek, *Beyond "Homophobia": A Social Psychological Perspective on Attitudes Toward Lesbians and Gay Men* (Binghamton, N.Y.: Haworth Press, 1984).

4. For over twenty years, I have been involved in a remarkable week-long training program in human sexuality. Participants from all walks of life explore the multiple dimensions of, and roadblocks to, sexual health. (See entry for Annual Workshop on Sexuality at Thornfield in Resources, "Sexual Health").

5. Brian McNaught, "Dear Anita, Late Night Thoughts of an Irish Catholic Homosexual," *On Being Gay* (New York: St. Martin's Press, 1988).

CHAPTER NINE
ABOUT RELIGION AND SPIRITUALITY

1. Joseph Campbell, *The Hero with a Thousand Faces,* 2d ed. (Princeton: Princeton University Press, 1968).

2. Edward Farrell, *Prayer Is a Hunger* (Denville, N.J.: Dimension Books, 1972).

3. Hermann Hesse, *Siddhartha,* tr. Hilda Rosner (New York: New Directions Books, 1951).

4. Joseph Campbell, *The Power of Myth* (New York: Doubleday, 1988).

5. Paul Monette, *Becoming a Man: Half a Life Story.* (New York: Harcourt Brace Jovanovich, 1992).

6. John Boswell, *Christianity, Social Tolerance, and Homosexuality: Gay People in Western Europe from the Beginning of the Christian Era to the Fourteenth Century* (Chicago: University of Chicago Press, 1980).

7. James Redfield, *The Celestine Prophecy* (New York: Warner Books, 1994).

8. Mark Thompson, ed. *Gay Soul* (San Francisco: HarperSan Francisco, 1994).

9. Marlo Morgan, *Mutant Message Down Under* (New York: HarperCollins, 1994).

10. Dan Millman, *The Way of the Peaceful Warrior,* rev. ed. (Tiburon, Cal.: H.J. Kramer, 1984).

11. Brian L. Weiss, *Many Lives, Many Masters* (New York: Simon & Schuster, 1988).

12. Codependents Anonymous (see entry for Alcoholics Anonymous World Services in Resources, "Support").

13. John McNeill, S.J., *The Church and the Homosexual* (Kansas City: Sheed Andrews and McMeel, 1976).

14. Anthony Kosnik, et al., *Human Sexuality, New Directions in American Catholic Thought: A Study Commissioned by the Catholic Theological Society of America* (New York: Paulist Press, 1977).

CHAPTER TEN
ABOUT ASSESSING THE OPTIONS

1. Rita Mae Brown, *Rubyfruit Jungle.* (Plainfield, Vt.: Daughters, Inc., 1973).

2. Armistead Maupin, *Tales of the City.* (New York: Harper & Row, 1978).

RESOURCES

The organizations and programs listed here are invaluable resources for gay, lesbian, bisexual, and transgender people and their heterosexual allies.

LEGAL

American Civil Liberties Union (ACLU)
National Gay and Lesbian Rights Project
132 West 43rd Street
New York, NY 10036
(212) 944-9800 (ext. 545)

Gay and Lesbian Advocates and Defenders (GLAD)
P.O. Box 218
Boston, MA 02112
(617) 426-1350

Lambda Legal Defense and Education Fund
666 Broadway
12th Floor
New York, NY 10012
(212) 995-8585

National Center for Lesbian Rights
870 Market Street
Suite 570
San Francisco, CA 94102
(415) 392-6257

National Lesbian and Gay Law Association
Box 77130
National Capital Station
Washington, DC 20014
(202) 389-0161

POLITICAL AND WORK-RELATED

Gay and Lesbian Alliance Against Defamation (GLAAD)
8455 Beverly Boulevard
Suite 305
Los Angeles, CA 90048
(213) 658-6775

Gay and Lesbian Victory Fund
1012 14th Street, NW
Suite 1000
Washington, DC 20005
(202) 842-8679

Hollywood Supports
6922 Hollywood Boulevard
Suite 1015
Los Angeles, CA 90028
(213) 468-1270

Human Rights Campaign (HRC)
1101 14th Street, NW
Suite 200
Washington, DC 20005
(202) 628-4160

National Gay and Lesbian Task Force (NGLTF)
2320 17th Street, NW

Washington, DC 20009-2702
(202) 332-6483

V Management, LLC
Howard Tharsing
151 Lakeside Drive
PH 1
Oakland, CA 94612
800-452-6291

Wall Street Project
P.O. Box 387
New York, NY 10028
(212) 289-1741

SEXUAL HEALTH

American Association of Sex Educators, Counselors, and
Therapists (AASECT)
P.O. Box 238
Mount Vernon, IA 52314
(319) 895-8407

Annual Workshop on Sexuality at Thornfield
3600 Hill Street
Fairfax, VA 22030-3004
(703) 591-7120

Planned Parenthood Federation of America
810 7th Avenue
New York, NY 10019
(212) 541-7800

Sexuality Information and Education Council of the United
States (SIECUS)
130 West 42nd Street
Suite 350
New York, NY 10036-7901
(212) 819-9770

SPIRITUAL

There are an abundant number of institutions, organizations,
and groups dedicated to supporting the spiritual interests of
gay, lesbian, bisexual, and transgender people. Too numerous to
list here, they include worshipping communities, caucuses, and
discussion groups for nearly every major religious belief,
denomination, or spiritual inclination. For an up-to-date listing
of these resources at both the national and local levels, see
Gayellow Pages, available in most bookstores or from Renaissance
House, P.O. Box 533, Village Station, New York, NY 10014-0533.

SUPPORT

Alcoholics Anonymous World Services
475 Riverside Drive
New York, NY 10115
(212) 870-3400

Campaign to End Homophobia
P.O. Box 438316
Chicago, IL 60643-8316
(617) 868-8280

Gay, Lesbian, and Straight Teachers Network (GLSTN)
122 West 26th Street

Suite 1100
New York, NY 10001
(212) 727-0135

Hetrick-Martin Institute
2 Astor Place
New York, NY 10003-6998
(212) 674-2400

New Ways Ministry
4012 29th Street
Mt. Rainier, MD 20712
(301) 277-5674

Parents, Families and Friends of Lesbians and Gays (P-FLAG)
1101 14th Street, NW
Suite 1030
Washington, DC 20005
(202) 638-4200

AIDS

AIDS Action Council
1875 Connecticut Avenue, NW
Suite 700
Washington, DC 20009
(202) 986-1300

American Foundation for AIDS Research (AmFAR)
733 Third Avenue
12th Floor
New York, NY 10017
(212) 682-7440

American Red Cross National Headquarters
430 17th Street, NW
Washington, DC 20006
(202) 737-8300

CDC (Centers for Disease Control) National AIDS and HIV
Hotline
(800) 342-AIDS
(800) 344-SIDA (Spanish)
(800) AIDS-TTY (hearing impaired)

CDC National AIDS Clearinghouse
(800) 458-5231 (to order materials)

National Leadership Coalition on AIDS
1730 M Street, NW
Suite 905
Washington, DC 20036
(202) 429-0930

TRANSGENDER ISSUES

International Foundation for Gender Education
123 Moody Street
Waltham, MA 02154
(617) 894-8340

Outreach Institute of Gender Studies
126 Western Avenue
Suite 246
Augusta, ME 04330
(207) 621-0858

Renaissance Education Association
987 Old Eagle School Road
Suite 719
Wayne, PA 19087
(610) 975-9119

MATERIAL SOURCES

Lambda Rising Bookstore
1625 Connecticut Avenue, NW
Washington, DC 20009-1013
(800) 621-6969

ABOUT THE AUTHOR

Brian McNaught has been an educator about homosexuality since 1974. He is the author of four books, has contributed to numerous nonfiction anthologies, and is featured in several popular educational videos, including some aired regularly on PBS stations. He consults for corporations on the issues facing gay employees and has spoken at over one hundred universities. From 1982 to 1984, he served as the Mayor of Boston's ombudsperson to the gay community.

Brian was born in Detroit, Michigan, in 1948. He received his B.A. in journalism from Marquette University in 1970, and is certified as a sexuality educator by the American Association of Sex Educators, Counselors, and Therapists (AASECT). He has received numerous citations for his work, including the Mary Lee Tatum Award from Planned Parenthood for his contribution to the public's understanding of homosexuality.

Brian and his life partner, Ray Struble, live in San Francisco, California, and in Provincetown, Massachusetts.